Britain in the Second World War

D0144120

The Second World War was the defining episode for twentieth-century history and indeed for much of the war Britain was by far the most important nation of the Allies. This book presents a new and vivid survey of politics, society, culture and military strategy between 1939 and 1945. Structured around themes such as 'Wartime Media', and 'Britain and its Allies', the book covers the major historical debates of these areas, including Britain's commitment to remain in the conflict until unconditional surrender and the effect of war on the status of women.

Britain in the Second World War includes discussion of:
* politics, including Churchill's wartime strategy and the 1945 election
* the economy
* 'selling' the war to the public
* the influence of war on British society

Britain in the Second World War is a compact history of wartime Britain which not only provides a succinct narrative of events, but also highlights contemporary historical debate.

Mark Donnelly is Director of History at St Mary's, Strawberry Hill.

Britain in the Second World War

Mark Donnelly

London and New York

First published 1999
by Routledge
11 New Fetter Lane, London EC4P 4EE

Simultaneously published in the USA and Canada
by Routledge
29 West 35th Street, New York, NY 10001

Routledge Ltd is an imprint of the Taylor & Francis Group

©1999 Mark Donnelly

Typeset in Baskerville by Routledge
Printed and bound in Great Britain by TJ International Ltd, Padstow,
Cornwall

British Library Cataloguing in Publication Data
A catalogue record for this book is available from the British Library

Library of Congress Cataloging in Publication Data
Britain in the Second World War/Mark Donnelly.
Includes bibliographical references and index.
1. World War, 1939–1945 – Great Britain.
2. Great Britain – Politics and government –
1936–1945. 3. Great Britain – History, Military
– 20th century. 4. Churchill, Winston, Sir, 1874–1965.
I. Title.
D759.D63 1999   99–11773
940.53'41–dc21   CIP

ISBN 0–415–17425–2 (hbk)
ISBN 0–415–17426–0 (pbk)

Contents

Acknowledgements

As this book is largely the product of teaching rather than research, my first thanks are to those students at St Mary's who have taken my course on Britain in the second world war. I would also like to thank Christopher Lehane, Christopher White, Patrick Hanlon and David Fish for their intelligent comments and advice. Sally Morley, Ann-Marie Hing and Maria Jeavons provided valuable support and I am grateful to the staff at Routledge – particularly Wendy Lees and Heather McCallum – for their help with this book. As always my greatest debt is to Joyce and Terry Donnelly, to whom this book is dedicated.

Abbreviations

BBC	British Broadcasting Corporation
BEF	British Expeditionary Force
CEMA	Council for the Encouragement of Music and the Arts
CPGB	Communist Party of Great Britain
EEC	European Economic Community
FBI	Federation of British Industry
GPO	General Post Office
ILP	Independent Labour Party
MOI	Ministry of Information
NATO	North Atlantic Treaty Organisation
NEC	National Executive Committee (Labour Party)
NHS	National Health Service
PLP	Parliamentary Labour Party
RAF	Royal Air Force
TGWU	Transport and General Workers' Union
TUC	Trades Union Congress
VE Day	Victory in Europe day
VJ Day	Victory over Japan day

Chronology of the war in the west

1939

1 September	Germans attack Poland.
3 September	Britain and France declare war on Germany.
17 September	USSR invades eastern Poland.
29 September	Surrender of Poland.

1940

8 April	British destroyers mine Norwegian waters around Narvik. German troops land in Norway – the first amphibious landing of the war. Germans overrun Denmark.
15–18 April	British, French and Polish troops land in Norway, at Narvik, Namsos and Andalsnes.
2 May	British troops evacuate Namsos and Andalsnes.
10 May	Germany launches its attack on the west across the frontiers of Holland, Belgium and Luxembourg.
13 May	German forces cross the Meuse.
14 May	Surrender of the Netherlands.
20 May	German forces reach the Channel ports.

26–8 May	War Cabinet discusses possibility of a negotiated settlement with Germany.
27 May	Calais falls and the evacuation of Allied troops from Dunkirk begins. Belgium surrenders.
4 June	Evacuation from Dunkirk completed.
10 June	Mussolini leads Italy into war against Britain and France.
14 June	Germans capture Paris.
22 June	French sign armistice with Germany and Italy. Britain supports General Charles de Gaulle as head of the French National Committee in London.
25 June	French armistice takes effect.
3 July	British warships attack the French fleet at Mers-el-Kebir.
10 July	Battle of Britain begins with German raids on dockyards and shipping.
13 August	Major German air raids begin on British airfields, factories and docks.
7 September	Blitz on London begins.
13 September	Italians attack British forces in Egypt.
17 September	Hitler postpones invasion of Britain after heavy losses are inflicted on the Luftwaffe.
7 October	German troops enter Romania.
12 October	Hitler abandons invasion plans for 1940.
28 October	Italians attack Greece.
9 December	British counter attack – Operation Compass – begins in Egypt.

1941

22 January	British forces take Libyan port of Tobruk.

12 February	General Rommel arrives at the Libyan port of Tripoli and soon reverses British gains in north Africa.
7 March	British forces arrive in Greece.
9 March	Italy attacks Greece.
11 March	Lend Lease Act approved in the US.
6 April	Greece and Yugoslavia attacked by Germany.
24 April	Greek forces surrender.
29 April	British forces complete their evacuation from Greece: some 20,000 troops are taken to Crete.
10 May	Rudolf Hess flies to Britain with suggested terms for peace.
20 May	German invasion of Crete.
1 June	British forces complete their evacuation from Crete.
21 June	Operation Barbarossa: Germany invades the Soviet Union.
9 August	Churchill and Roosevelt meet for the first time during the war at Placentia Bay.
12 August	Atlantic Charter signed by Churchill and Roosevelt.
25 August	British and Soviet forces enter Persia (Iran).
7 December	Japanese forces attack US naval base at Pearl Harbor, Hawaii.
11 December	Germany and Italy declare war on US.
22 December–3 January 1942	Arcadia Conference at Washington confirms 'Germany first' strategy.

1942

17 June	British forces withdraw from Libya.
21 June	British forces surrender at Tobruk.
28 June	German armies in the east launch a summer offensive in the Caucasus.

24 July	British and US strategists agree to open a second front in north Africa rather than Europe.
19 August	Allied raid on Dieppe ends in disaster.
10 September	German troops enter Stalingrad.
23 October–4 November	Battle of El Alamein ends in victory for Allies.
8 November	Operation Torch: Anglo-US invasion of Vichy-controlled north Africa.
11 November	Resistance of Vichy French forces to Anglo-US landings in north Africa ceases.
13 November	Allies recapture Tobruk.
19 November	Soviet forces begin their counter attack at Stalingrad.

1943

January	Casablanca Conference: western Allies agree that the invasion of Sicily and mainland Italy will follow the securing of north Africa. Roosevelt announces that the Allies will seek the unconditional surrender of the enemy.
2 February	German forces surrender at Stalingrad.
March	Allied shipping losses in Atlantic peak.
11 May	Axis forces surrender in Tunisia.
21 May	Trident Conference in Washington sets date for Anglo-US landings in Europe in 1944.
23 May	Admiral Dönitz withdraws U-boats from Atlantic as Allies use long-range bombers and improvements in radar to gain clear combat advantage.
10 July	Allies invade Sicily.

25 July	Fall of Mussolini's regime in Italy. Marshal Badoglio forms a new government.
18 August	Collapse of German resistance in Sicily.
3 September	Allied troops cross to the Italian mainland. Allies sign armistice with the Badoglio regime.
8 September	Italians surrender to the Allies.
15 September	Mussolini declares a new fascist regime in northern Italy after his rescue by German troops.
1 October	Allies enter Naples.
13 October	Italy declares war on Germany.

1944

22 January	Allied landings at Anzio, south of Rome.
4 June	Allies enter Rome.
6 June	D-Day landings in Normandy.
13 June	First V-1 raid on London.
22 June	Soviets launch massive offensive in the east.
26 June	Allied troops take port of Cherbourg.
9 July	Allied troops take Caen.
20 July	Stauffenberg bomb plot fails to kill Hitler at Rastenberg.
6 August	Germans launch counter-offensive at Mortain.
15 August	Operation Anvil/Dragoon: Allied troops land in French Riviera.
25 August	Allies liberate Paris.
3 September	Allies take Brussels and Lyons.
8 September	First V-2 rockets land on southern England.
15 September	At the Quebec Conference, Churchill and Roosevelt agree the Morgenthau Plan: a programme to convert Germany into a primarily pastoral and agricultural country.

17–25 September	Operation Market Garden: Allied attempt to secure crossings over major Dutch rivers ends in failure at Arnhem.
16–25 December	The Battle of the Bulge: German counter-offensive at Ardennes.

1945

17 January	Soviets take Warsaw.
4 February	Yalta Conference begins: Allies confirm plans to partition post-war Germany.
7 March	US troops cross the Rhine at Remagen.
12 April	US President Roosevelt dies.
28 April	Mussolini shot dead by communist partisans.
30 April	Hitler commits suicide in his Berlin bunker.
2 May	Formal surrender of Germans in Italy.
7 May	German forces surrender unconditionally.
8 May	'VE Day': Victory in Europe Day.
6 August	Atomic bomb dropped on Hiroshima.
8 August	USSR declares war on Japan.
9 August	Atomic bomb dropped on Nagasaki.
14 August	Japanese accept Allied surrender terms.
15 August	'VJ Day': Victory over Japan Day celebrated in Britain.

Introduction

It remains the most striking paradox in contemporary British history: a global conflict which killed some 60 million and which left the legacy of Auschwitz, Hiroshima and countless acts of barbarism has evoked nostalgia, pride and even sentimentality in Britain for over fifty years. In one sense the paradox is simple to understand. Popular perceptions of the second world war have been filtered through the unique experience of the British from 1939 to 1945: relatively light casualties, no invasion of the home islands, standing alone as the only major power against Germany after the fall of France, a propaganda campaign which emphasised both the communal nature of the 'people's war' and the moral superiority of the national cause, and victory as the only member of the 'Big Three' to have fought from the outset.

Britain of course was not alone in creating a myth of the second world war experience: the French myth privileged the role of the Resistance in the struggle against Nazi occupation; the Soviets remembered the Great Patriotic War against fascism; the United States took great pride in the extraordinary feats of production which saw America transformed into the 'arsenal of democracy'. Nevertheless, the existence of a British national myth which retained such power for so long raises important questions about the way in which the conflict and its legacy have been historicised in Britain.

More generally, perhaps, the myth of the war years also raises questions about the challenge faced by historians who write about the recent past. Interpretations of the war coloured by sentiment are not confined to folklore, popular journalism or television documentaries. They can be found in much of the British historiography produced since the conflict ended. Not surprisingly, the generation of historians who experienced the war as adults frequently emphasised the heroic nature of the war effort and identified the conflict as a turning point in

British history. For example, Richard Titmuss argued that the war produced a heightened sense of social solidarity at home which in turn led to the adoption of egalitarian social policies during and after the conflict (Titmuss 1950). Charles Mowat claimed that the British 'found themselves' again in the summer of 1940 and resolved to face the future with renewed determination (Mowat 1955: 657). A. J. P. Taylor argued in similar vein that the British people 'came of age' during the war, exchanging a commitment to imperial greatness for a commitment to welfare reform and a drive to improve social conditions (Taylor 1965: 600).

Where these commentators led, others followed, until by the 1970s a composite picture of the 'good' war had emerged. The heroism and self-sacrifice of Dunkirk and the 'finest hour'; the valour of the Eighth Army in north Africa; the liberation of western Europe after D-Day; the inspired leadership of Churchill; the new political consensus forged by the wartime coalition government; the triumph of communal values in Labour's election victory of 1945 – all of these featured in the traditional version of the war. But as more archival material became available and a generation of historians who were born after the war began to write about the conflict with more critical detachment, a different picture took shape. It was a picture that was far less comforting. According to revisionist versions of the war the home front was marked by social division, class-based resentment, racial discrimination and rising crime rates; the ideological divisions between the main political parties remained as pronounced as ever by 1945; Labour won the 1945 election primarily because it was less unpopular than the Tories; Churchill was an error-prone maverick whose mishandling of strategy hindered the war effort; and the price of victory in 1945 was simply too high – Britain, it has been argued, should have taken the opportunity to conclude a compromise peace with Hitler in 1941.

The following chapters will examine these issues and other interpretations of Britain's experience of the second world war. The approach is thematic – politics, society, economy, media and strategy – and each chapter is based on secondary sources rather than archival research. No attempt has been made at sustained comparative analysis, because the main purpose of the book is to introduce the major historiographical debates about Britain's experience of the war, and most of the historiography produced in Britain in this field is not comparative. The literature surveyed here is written largely by British historians – of course there is a massive collection of texts on the war produced by scholars across the world, but to survey that collection would require a very different, and much longer, book. A bibliography containing all the works referred to in this text is included: it is intended as a useful guide for further reading, but it represents only a fraction of the literature available.

Chapter 1

Wartime politics

The most significant political developments in Britain during the second world war followed the formation of a new coalition government under Winston Churchill in May 1940. This coalition replaced the Conservative-dominated national government which had been in power since 1931, thereby ending a decade of Conservative ascendancy. Labour returned to a share in government with fewer posts than the Conservatives, but historians have shown that the party used its place in the coalition to reshape the domestic agenda of British politics (Addison 1975; Jefferys 1991; Brooke 1992). At the administrative level, the functions of government simply grew to meet the demands of 'total war'. The staff of central government almost doubled in wartime and new methods of economic management, industrial organisation and public administration were used, some of which lasted into the post-war period (see chapter 3). At the popular level, the common experience of war was seen by commentators to have promoted a new set of political values. It is generally agreed that the wartime 'swing to the left' contributed to the election of the first majority Labour government in 1945; as will be shown, however, the debate continues about the strength, timing and ideological content of this shift in political opinion (Mason and Thompson 1991; Fielding 1992). More controversial still is the thesis that cross-party co-operation in wartime gave rise to a political consensus, characterised by policy convergence on areas such as welfare reform, the operation of a mixed economy, conciliation of the trade unions and a commitment to full employment (Addison 1975; Kavanagh and Morris 1994; Dutton 1997b). This chapter will assess the political impact of the war, both at Westminster and in terms of popular attitudes. First, though, a brief discussion is required of high politics in the immediate pre-war period and the factors which led to the replacement of Chamberlain's government with Churchill's coalition.

The outbreak of war and the downfall of Chamberlain

The declaration of war on Germany on 3 September 1939 was announced by Neville Chamberlain, a forceful if uncharismatic Conservative politician who succeeded Stanley Baldwin as Prime Minister in May 1937. Chamberlain's arrival at the top of the political hierarchy coincided with an acceleration in Britain's recovery from the deep and prolonged depression which had scarred parts of the country during the inter-war years. He could claim some credit for this as a former Chancellor in a government which combined low interest rates, a managed exchange rate, balanced budgets – or at worst modest budget deficits – cautious social reform and limited state intervention in industry to ease recovery. As Prime Minister, though, Chamberlain's attention was diverted away from the domestic issues which had preoccupied him at the Treasury and towards the sphere of international diplomacy.

Chamberlain had the misfortune to become premier at a time when a second major war in twenty years appeared likely. Germany had never been reconciled to the punitive conditions and territorial losses imposed in 1919 after its defeat in the first world war. When Adolf Hitler's National Socialist Party came to power in 1933 there was no longer any doubt that Germany was prepared to use force to secure a revision of the post-war settlement in its favour. Germany was joined in its rejection of the legitimacy of the 1919 settlement by Italy, ruled since 1922 by the fascist dictator Benito Mussolini. Lacking the resources to realise their own territorial ambitions in isolation, the Italians welcomed the prospect of a militarily powerful Germany challenging Britain and France, the two main guarantors of stability in the Mediterranean. Outside Europe, Japan was a third major power committed to a policy of territorial expansion. As part of its objective of increasing its economic, strategic and military power in the Pacific, Japan occupied the Chinese territory of Manchuria in 1931 and further encroached into northern China in 1937. By the time he became Prime Minister, therefore, Chamberlain was faced with three powers which were prepared to go to war in pursuit of their foreign policy goals and who threatened Britain's interests in Europe and Asia.

Chamberlain believed that he could save Britain from war by acting as a diplomatic broker, maintaining peace by redressing grievances with negotiation and compromise. In the 1930s this policy of appeasement was supported by the Chiefs of Staff who warned that Britain would lose a war against Germany, Italy and Japan unless it had the support of the United States. In addition to the strategic rationale for appeasement, supporters of the policy also used political, economic and moral arguments to justify their position. Many of these arguments are contentious, but the point remains that Chamberlain's conduct of foreign policy consolidated rather than weakened his authority before the war. Even as potentially damaging an episode as the resignation of his Foreign Secretary, Anthony Eden, after a disagreement over policy towards Italy in February 1938, was met with broad equanimity by press and politicians. In view of the opprobrium which was later heaped on Chamberlain, Lord Halifax – Eden's successor at the Foreign Office – and his cabinet colleagues, Sir John Simon and Samuel Hoare, it should also be remembered that appeasement was accompanied by rearmament, particularly of Britain's air defences. Appeasement was not a strategy to buy time, but Chamberlain and his advisers always recognised the need to prepare the country for conflict in case negotiated settlements of international disputes proved unobtainable. The worth of this policy was proved in the aftermath of the Czech crisis of September 1938, as the realisation set in that a peaceful way of satisfying Germany's ambitions was a chimera.

It now appears that Hitler was determined to provoke war with Czechoslovakia in preparation for a later attack on the Soviet Union. But the ostensible issue in the autumn of 1938 was the fate of some three million German-speaking Sudetendeutsche within the Czech borders, whom Hitler demanded should be included within his Reich. Chamberlain took this demand at face value and began the search for a peaceful resolution of the Czech–German border dispute. Despite the fact that the Czechs could put between thirty and forty divisions in the field, had a heavily fortified mountain frontier with Germany and possessed the largest armaments factory in the world, Britain recommended that frontier areas which contained a German majority should be given full and immediate rights of self-determination. Chamberlain flew to a series of meetings with Hitler to broker a settlement, while at the same time co-ordinating policy with the French and keeping up the pressure on the Czech President Benes to sacrifice land for peace. The product of these efforts was the Munich Agreement, which transferred the Sudetenland to Germany under international supervision and averted war. The Agreement was met with public euphoria in Britain, most of the press regarded it as a triumph for Chamberlain and it was endorsed by a large majority in the Commons. Nevertheless, euphoria was soon overtaken by an awkward recognition that the Czechs had been forced to make a sacrifice which effectively destroyed their strategic integrity. Nagging doubts also remained that Hitler was far from satiated and that war had been delayed rather than averted.

The Munich Agreement and Hitler's assurances that he would respect the new Czech frontiers proved worthless in March 1939 when German forces occupied Prague and what remained of the Czech provinces of Czechoslovakia. Acknowledging that previous peaceful attempts to restrain Hitler had failed, Britain resolved to send a clear signal to Germany that it would not remain neutral if another nation's sovereignty was violated. This attempt to restrain Germany with a threat of force took the specific form of a guarantee to Poland; this was of limited value to the Poles without a concomitant agreement with the Soviet Union, but the ultimate purpose was to leave Hitler in no doubt about Britain's intentions. In the spring and summer of 1939 Britain made preparations for a war that was increasingly unavoidable; rearmament was accelerated, air-raid shelters were built and conscription began. The signing of the Nazi–Soviet pact on 23 August 1939 left Hitler with a free hand to attack Poland and cleared the way for war. After attempts to secure British neutrality had failed, the Germans attacked Poland on 1 September. Chamberlain, who had invested so much on the preservation of peace, now had to lead his country in war.

Much has been made of Chamberlain's apparent unsuitability as a wartime leader. Two of his earliest biographers argued that he was simply not the right man to lead the country in war and that his replacement was only a matter of time (Feiling 1970: 419; Macleod 1961: 282). Taylor argued that Chamberlain never fully recovered his authority after the abandonment of appeasement and ultimately paid the price in May 1940 (Taylor 1965). This deterministic view of Chamberlain's downfall, though, has been challenged by writers who argue that it was avoidable mistakes made by the Prime Minister after rather than before the outbreak of war which were crucial (Jefferys 1991; Corfield 1996). The failure to preserve peace was undoubtedly a blow to Chamberlain on a number of different levels, but there was nothing inevitable about his replacement by Churchill after appeasement had given way to war. Chamberlain had the opportunity to re-establish his political authority during the early phase of the war, but he spurned the chance.

Chamberlain's delay in sending an ultimatum to Germany after their attack on Poland was not without justification; careful arrangements with Britain's main ally, France, had to be agreed and whenever the announcement of war came there was no prospect of Britain lending actual military support to the Poles. Nevertheless, the fact that the ultimatum and declaration of war were held back until 3 September raised suspicions that Chamberlain was intent on a further deal with Hitler and left the impression that the Prime Minister had been reluctantly dragged into war after having seriously considered reneging on Britain's guarantee to Poland. Cabinet and parliament had both expressed strong opposition to the delay and it was no surprise when the All-Party Parliamentary Action Group was formed – chaired by the Liberal, Clement Davies – to keep a watchful eye over the government's conduct of the war.

For those at Westminster who doubted the Prime Minister's capabilities as a war leader, though, there seemed no immediate prospect of his removal. Chamberlain minimised the prospect of a revolt from within his party by including two of his most high-profile critics inside the government: Churchill came into the nine-man war cabinet as First Lord of the Admiralty and Eden was appointed to the non-cabinet post of Dominions Secretary. Chamberlain's government enjoyed a safe majority of more than 200 in parliament; the three main parties signed an electoral truce in which they agreed not to contest the previous incumbent's party at by-elections; the national press at the start of the war believed it had a patriotic duty to support the Prime Minister; and opinion polls by November 1939 showed that Chamberlain was more popular than ever. Apart from a handful of pacifists at Westminster, the Independent Labour Party (ILP) and eventually the Communist Party of Great Britain (CPGB), there was little organised opposition to the war effort. The Labour Party, which had long advocated a more forceful stance against Hitler, refused Chamberlain's invitation to join his government and opted instead for a position of 'patriotic opposition'. In the long term this refusal was to have profoundly damaging consequences for the Prime Minister, but in the context of September 1939 it raised more difficulties for Labour than for Chamberlain. The party reserved the right to criticise the war effort, but the line between criticism and disloyalty to the national cause at a time of emergency was a thin one which had to be walked carefully.

It was in the early months of hostilities that Chamberlain undermined his position of strength and built up the well of resentment, mistrust and dissatisfaction which was to prove crucial in May 1940.

Despite Hitler's offensives against Czechoslovakia and Poland, the Prime Minister continued to believe from September 1939 that a major war could be averted in Europe; the longer the Germans delayed their attack on the west, the more convinced Chamberlain became that they had 'missed the bus' and would not risk a war against British and French forces which had been allowed time to rearm. The navy carried the fight to the enemy, sinking German U-boats , forcing the scuttling of the German pocket battleship *Graf Spee* in December 1939, and seizing the *Altmark* in February 1940. But the army was involved in no major action on land before April 1940 and the Royal Air Force (RAF) had to be content with dropping propaganda leaflets rather than explosives over Germany. With some insensitivity to those seamen who fought and died at the time, the early months of the conflict became known as the 'bore war', later the 'phoney war'. As Chamberlain's conviction grew that a major campaign could be avoided, he saw no need to galvanise the country, his administration or the economy fully for war. This was the misjudgement which ultimately made his position as Prime Minister untenable.

Criticisms of Chamberlain's command of the war effort can be divided into two broad categories. The first was his handling of personnel; here he was accused of promoting known government loyalists to important posts rather than individuals with talent and ability (Addison 1975: 66; Jefferys 1991: 18). Chamberlain's Chief Whip, David Margesson, ensured that the old inner-ring who had dominated government in the pre-war period held on to power; with the exception of Churchill, this meant that no member of the cabinet was forceful enough to rival the authority of Chamberlain in the Commons. The Prime Minister's political instincts and the calculation that it was easier to divide and rule a larger cabinet may also help to explain why Chamberlain consistently rejected calls for a smaller, non-departmental war cabinet along the lines which Lloyd George had formed in the first world war. This refusal was blamed in part for the lacklustre organisation of the war effort in the early months. Critics hoped that as Asquith had been forced to give way to Lloyd George as premier in 1916, so too would Chamberlain be forced to stand aside for a more dynamic successor sooner rather than later.

The second major criticism of Chamberlain concerned his handling of the wartime economy. A series of measures were taken to mobilise the national resources for war: the distribution of manpower between the armed forces and key industries and services was controlled; targets were set for the expansion of war-related industries; new Ministries of

Supply and Food were established; and taxes were raised to help finance the war effort and check inflation. But critics focused on the government's failure to exert more wide-ranging state direction of the economy. There was particular disappointment at Chamberlain's refusal to create a new post in the war cabinet with overall responsibility for co-ordinating the war economy, supported by an economic general staff. Instead, control of the war economy was diffused across a range of separate departments. Aided by some helpful leaks from sympathetic civil servants, Labour made detailed and often effective attacks on inefficient ministries and continued to demand greater drive, planning and vision from the government. The opposition's charge of administrative complacency increasingly centred on the government's failure to tackle manpower shortages in key industries. Almost a million workers remained unemployed by spring 1940, yet many factories were working well below full capacity, there was a scarcity of skilled labour in some regions such as the Midlands, and Churchill complained in cabinet that organisation of manpower had barely begun in the engineering, motor and aircraft manufacturing industries (Corfield 1996: 22–8). These manpower shortages contributed to wage inflation and poaching of labour; more significantly, they acted as a brake on the expansion of industries which were vital to the war effort. To tackle the problem effectively required a fundamental restructuring of labour-supply policy, which in turn implied close co-operation between government and trade unions. Chamberlain's administration, however, was only prepared to consult the trade unions, it was not willing to recognise a formal role for them in the management of the war effort. Ernest Bevin, the General Secretary of the Transport and General Workers' Union (TGWU), argued that the successful prosecution of the war required an effective partnership between government, employers and unions; he concluded publicly on May Day 1940 that only a new government could construct such a partnership.

Bevin was not alone in his belief that the early months of the war had demonstrated the need for a new government. Since September 1939 Labour had been willing in principle to join a coalition government, provided they were allocated a sufficient share in power, and as the war progressed their conviction grew that a government of national unity was vital; their main objection was to serving under Chamberlain, whom they regarded as having built up a charge sheet of offences against the Labour movement which was too long to be ignored (Addison 1975: 54). Members of the backbench All-Party Parliamentary Action Group shared the view that the time had come to replace an administration that had run its course. Chamberlain's most vehement critics simply had to wait for an opportunity to strike a fatal blow against his leadership; when British forces failed in their first major offensive of the war in Norway in April and May 1940 their moment had arrived.

Chamberlain was not primarily responsible for the chaos which led to the evacuation of the British Expeditionary Force (BEF) from Norway – Churchill had a far more direct role in its planning and execution – but the episode came to be seen as a manifestation of the deeper malaise which the Prime Minister's consistent failures of leadership since the outbreak of war had produced. Labour's response to the defeat was to initiate a two-day debate on the conduct of the war on 7 and 8 May; it was this debate which sealed Chamberlain's fate as Prime Minister.

The details of the debate have been recounted frequently elsewhere (Addison 1975: 94–8; Jefferys 1991: 22–4; Roberts 1976), so a brief summary will suffice here. On the first day of the debate, forceful contributions from Admiral Sir Roger Keyes and Leo Amery damaged the government and strengthened the resolve of critics, particularly on the Conservative benches, to act against Chamberlain. Amery's devastating critique carried extra force because he was a former colleague of the Prime Minister. His attack concluded with a rhetorical flourish which recalled Oliver Cromwell's injunction to the Long Parliament: 'You have sat too long here for any good you have been doing. Depart, I say, and let us have done with you. In the name of God, go.' At the beginning of the second day Labour announced that it would force a vote at the end of the debate; the party's initial fears that a division would persuade even critical Tories to rally behind their Prime Minister subsided as the strength of feeling against the government became apparent. Chamberlain compounded his problems by appealing to his 'friends' to support him in the division, leading perhaps unfairly to the accusation that he was attempting to transform an issue of national importance into a test of personal loyalty; it was after all common practice for members of parliament to refer to party colleagues as 'honourable friends'. Behind the scenes, Clement Davies and the All-Party Parliamentary Action Group cajoled and co-ordinated opposition to the Prime Minister. Finally, when the division was called on 8 May, Chamberlain fatally lacked the reservoir of goodwill and trust which Churchill was able to draw from after more serious military setbacks later in the war. The result of 281 votes for the government and 200 against was a victory for Chamberlain, but 40 members of his own party had voted against him and perhaps another 30 had abstained. After a brief and failed attempt to reconstruct his administration – during which Labour reaffirmed their refusal to serve under him – Chamberlain was forced to concede that a Prime Minister in a major war required a far greater endorsement from his colleagues than the one he had received. He resigned on 10 May, the same day that Hitler launched his attack on the west.

The myth which surrounds Churchill's role in the second world war suggests that he was the obvious and natural successor to Chamberlain. Churchill's own memoirs – which have done so much to shape and sustain the myth – put forward the view that he was 'walking with destiny' in May 1940 (Churchill 1948: 428). There can be little doubt that he was regarded in most quarters by this time as a contender for the premiership. His warnings in the 1930s about the dangers posed by Nazi Germany were now seen to be justified; he had long experience of parliament, government and high office; as First Lord of the Admiralty his dynamism, oratorical powers and flair for public relations easily eclipsed the efforts of all other ministers; and his support within Fleet Street ensured that he remained popular with the public. Against these qualities, though, had to be set obvious weaknesses which cast some doubt on his chances of succeeding Chamberlain. After crossing the floor of the House of Commons twice and alienating the Tory leadership on a range of personal and political matters, Churchill had been kept out of office in the 1930s and lacked a solid base of support within his party. His temperament was seen by many as too volatile for the position of Prime Minister – a view which was reinforced by his conduct at the Admiralty which reawakened memories of the daring but ultimately disastrous Dardanelles operation of 1915. Senior civil servants shivered at the prospect of Churchill leading a government, a sense of unease that was shared by King George VI who remembered Churchill's support for Edward VIII in the Abdication crisis (Roberts 1994: 38–9). In fact, the choice of the monarchy, senior civil servants and Chamberlain himself to take over as Prime Minister was Lord Halifax. But at a meeting with Chamberlain, Churchill and Margesson on 9 May, Halifax ruled himself out of the job, ostensibly because he was reluctant to lead a government as a peer rather than an elected member of parliament, but more likely because he believed he could best act as a restraining force on Churchill from a senior but subordinate role within the war cabinet (Roberts 1992: 198–207). As a result, Churchill was asked to form a government on 10 May.

The Churchill coalition, 1940–2

Churchill had become Prime Minister largely because members of all the main parties were prepared to serve under him in a coalition, not because he was seen as a national saviour. The popularity and political authority which he enjoyed later in the war often overshadows the extent to which Churchill's position was constrained in the early months of his premiership. Although Chamberlain was now a subordinate in Churchill's war cabinet, he remained the leader of the Conservative party at Westminster, most of whom had stayed loyal during the two-day debate. Among those Tories who had deserted Chamberlain on 8 May was a number who regretted their rebellion almost immediately; their aim had been to register a protest at the government's performance, not to force the resignation of the Prime Minister. When Churchill first entered the Commons as Prime Minister on 13 May he was greeted by silence on the Conservative benches, Chamberlain in contrast received an ovation. The new Prime Minister had to wait some time before winning over the doubters in his own party (Roberts 1994: 137–210).

From the outset Churchill was aware of the need to retain a degree of party balance in his appointments to cabinet and government. His first war cabinet contained two senior Conservatives – Chamberlain as Lord President of the Council and Halifax as Foreign Secretary – and the leader and deputy leader of the Labour party – Clement Attlee as Lord Privy Seal and Arthur Greenwood as Minister without Portfolio. Also, the three service ministries were divided between representatives of each of the main parties. Overall, though, the Conservatives retained a numerical superiority in the government, due largely to the insistence of Margesson that the administration should reflect the Tories' majority at Westminster. Labour welcomed the opportunity to participate in government for the first time since 1931, but they received less than one-third of all posts in the coalition. Margesson's continued presence as Chief Whip also helped to ensure that two-thirds of Chamberlain's old administration survived the arrival of Churchill as Prime Minister. Although he was leader of a coalition, the lack of a solid party political base of his own was a potential danger for Churchill and he was aware of the need to retain the support of his fellow Tories in the war cabinet; if Chamberlain and Halifax endorsed him, most of the party would follow. The new Prime Minister was also careful to ensure that Chamberlainites received sufficient government posts to keep them satisfied, but not so many that they controlled his ministry. Above all else, Churchill was determined to retain command of military strategy.

Churchill's authority in parliament and in the country was consolidated in the summer of 1940, the time when Britain and its Commonwealth allies began their lone stand against Germany following the surrender of the French in June. With the prospects of survival let alone victory in some jeopardy, Churchill employed all his oratorical talents in a series of defiant speeches which ignored the reality of Britain's strategic position. In place of compromise and appeasement, Churchill now offered 'victory at all costs'. In his first speech to the Commons as Prime Minister on 13 May, Churchill came out fighting:

> You ask, what is our aim? I can answer in one word. It is victory, victory at all costs, victory in spite of all terror, victory, however long and hard the road may be; for without victory, there is no survival. Let that be realised; no survival for the British Empire, no survival for all that the British Empire has stood for, no survival for the urge and impulse of the ages, that mankind will move forward towards its goal.

On 4 June, after the greater part of the British Expeditionary Force had been evacuated from Dunkirk, Churchill again stood unbowed and defiant in the House, determined to stare down an enemy which had swept aside all challengers thus far:

> We shall go on to the end, we shall fight in France, we shall fight on the seas and the oceans, we shall fight with growing confidence and growing strength in the air, we shall defend our island, whatever the cost may be, we shall fight on the beaches, we shall fight on the landing grounds, we shall fight in the fields and in the streets, we shall fight in the hills; we shall never surrender.

It was this defiance during the 'finest hour' that forged a bond between Churchill and people and began the myth of Churchill as the saviour of the nation. The defiance, though, was not for public consumption alone; in a series of meetings of the war cabinet on 26–8 May, Churchill carefully rejected the view of Halifax and Chamberlain that Britain should consider a negotiated peace with Germany (see chapter 5). Anxious to prevent the resignation of his Foreign Secretary, who pushed the case for a compromise peace hardest, Churchill claimed he had no principled objections to a negotiated settlement, he simply believed that Britain must improve its bargaining position before conducting any further dialogue with Hitler – at the very least it had to prove it could resist invasion. This was a shrewd position to adopt for the purpose of holding the war cabinet together, but in reality Churchill was never likely to accept a negotiated peace as a worthwhile goal. For him, the purpose of the war was the destruction of Nazism and he was not prepared to bargain away his role in the fulfilment of such a historic mission.

Churchill's need to maintain the support of Halifax and Chamberlain was reduced in the aftermath of the evacuation of the BEF from Dunkirk in June 1940. Led by critics in the press and the anonymous authors of the pamphlet *Guilty Men*, popular opinion after Dunkirk blamed the 'old gang' of Chamberlainites and appeasers for their apparent failure to prepare Britain adequately for war. Chamberlain offered his resignation, but Churchill refused. He was still unwilling to have the leader of the Conservatives outside his government, but by 30 July Churchill at least felt confident enough to declare that no competitor now threatened his position (Gilbert 1983: 697). Throughout the summer months, as Britain prepared to meet the expected German invasion, as the RAF fought the Battle of Britain, and as the blitz began in September, popular opinion and colleagues in parliament rallied behind Churchill. Chamberlain's retirement due to illness in October was a further advantage for the Prime Minister. It left him with more freedom to construct the government of his choice; more significantly, it opened the door for Churchill to become leader of the Conservatives, providing him at last with a bedrock of party support at Westminster. When Chamberlain's illness proved fatal in November, Churchill appointed Halifax as Britain's ambassador to Washington and replaced him at the Foreign Office with Anthony Eden. This confirmed that Churchill was now confident enough to break free from the constraints of May 1940; it also signalled that Eden, who had built up a following in the Tory party, wished to be the Prime Minister's heir rather than rival.

Churchill's enhanced prestige and authority did not mean that his leadership or his administration were immune from criticism. Throughout 1941 the Prime Minister's promises of victory began to sound increasingly hollow as British forces were overpowered in Crete, Greece and north Africa and heavy shipping losses continued in the Atlantic. Complaints surfaced about the Prime Minister's irregular working methods, erratic behaviour and tendency to dominate suppliant colleagues. More serious questions were asked about the strategic direction and organisation of the war effort, in particular the way in which production difficulties were seen to be impeding the effectiveness of the military. The main political consequences of this were twofold. First, it threw into sharp relief the ideological differences between the main coalition partners over the management of the war economy. Many within the Labour Party believed that socialist measures were essential in the drive to maximise production, but the Conservative-dominated coalition consistently rejected calls for nationalisation of coal mining, inland transport and the armaments industries, thereby confirming that Labour could expect to win only limited economic reforms from its participation in the coalition (Jefferys 1991: 66–77; Brooke 1992: 80–5). Second, the combination of military defeats and failures in war production led to suggestions that Churchill, who was both Prime Minister and Minister of Defence, should be relieved of the double burden of directing military strategy and overseeing the war on the home front.

Ironically, the two episodes which were to ensure Britain's eventual victory exacerbated these short-term political difficulties. Hitler's invasion of the Soviet Union in June 1941 created supply problems because additional material was required to support the new Russian allies; and Japan's entry into the war the following December led to a series of British defeats in the Far East which undermined morale and posed a threat to India. It was in this context that rivals of various calibre emerged to challenge Churchill's dominant hold on the direction of the war effort. Some, such as the Australian premier Robert Menzies and the Canadian Lord Beaverbrook, lacked sufficient support in parliament to mount an effective challenge. Eden, who privately grumbled that the Prime Minister was a hindrance to the war effort, had support in the Tory Party, but he had already tied his political fortunes to the continued patronage of Churchill. Stafford Cripps, though, was a rival of different quality. Regarded in some quarters, but chiefly by himself, as a potential Prime Minister, Cripps came to public attention at the beginning of 1942, the year in which lack of confidence in Churchill's particular brand of one-man government became acute.

Cripps had gained some public attention for his pre-war advocacy of a Popular Front against fascism, a campaign which saw him expelled from the Labour Party in January 1939. His political authority, though, was built mainly during his time as ambassador to Moscow in 1940–2. Cripps's absence from the country during this period freed him from any association with the defeats and failures which now threatened to undermine the position of Churchill. His campaign for a Second Front in Europe to aid the Soviets also meant that for a time he enjoyed the support of Lord Beaverbrook, member of the war cabinet and owner of several newspaper titles. Opinion polls showed that Cripps was increasingly regarded as a new figure who could bring greater urgency and efficiency to the war effort on the home front; the significance of this was not lost on Churchill, whose strategy was to restrain Cripps by persuading him to accept responsibility within the government. Cripps held out for a cabinet position and after the fall of Singapore in February was 'rewarded' with the posts of Lord Privy Seal and Leader of the House. He had his place in the war cabinet, but not in a position from which he could make a decisive impact; Churchill appeared to have given ground to his critics by appointing Cripps, in truth his control of the war effort remained as powerful as ever.

The Prime Minister's political acumen had bought his leadership some welcome breathing space. Cripps had responsibility but limited power and was soon despatched to India on an almost impossible mission to persuade the Congress Party to support Britain's war effort. Eden's loyalty, meanwhile, was encouraged by well-placed assurances that he was the natural heir if the Prime Minister was unable to continue in office; Eden was unlikely to risk a strike against Churchill so long as he believed that patience would deliver power into his hands. This loyalty from his Foreign Secretary was a useful asset for Churchill after the fall of the north African fortress of Tobruk in June 1942, a defeat that was as disastrous as it was unexpected. Tobruk was a low point in the war for Churchill and it brought renewed calls for a reduction of his powers and a restructuring of the government. With Eden's loyalty assured the only possible direct challenger to the Prime Minister was Cripps, a much less appealing figure for many Tories. Churchill was also fortunate that with critics such as Sir John Wardlaw-Milne in parliament he had scant need of friends. Supporting his own motion of no confidence in a debate on the conduct of the war in June, Wardlaw-Milne made the bizarre suggestion that the Duke of Gloucester might be made Commander-in-Chief of British forces. Aneurin Bevan, the backbench Labour MP who was Churchill's chief tormentor in parliament, did his best to infuse some substance into the case against the government, but the cause was already doomed by the derision which had met the earlier contributions of Wardlaw-Milne and others. The government defeated the censure motion by 475 to 25 votes, with about 30 abstentions. Churchill was relieved, but he was also aware that victory in debate counted for little unless it was matched soon by victory on the battlefield.

It was the wait for such a victory in the autumn of 1942 which Churchill later described as his most anxious period of the war. Stalin, senior US strategists and campaigners in Britain all expressed disappointment that Churchill had rejected an early invasion of Europe in favour of landings in north Africa; if this plan failed it was difficult to see how Churchill's position could remain tenable. Calculating that further military defeats had to result in a surrender of authority by the Prime Minister, Cripps decided that the time had come to apply some pressure of his own. In September Cripps presented his demand for an overhaul of the government apparatus, threatening resignation if his case was ignored. Churchill persuaded him to delay action until the result of the operation in north Africa was known; he conceded that if the landings failed there would have to be a fundamental change of direction, probably with a new leader. Once again, however, fortune favoured Churchill; news of General Montgomery's successful offensive at El Alamein in Egypt was followed by confirmation of the success of the Allied landings at Casablanca, Oran and Algiers on 8 November. Churchill at last had the major victory he needed to vindicate his handling of strategy. Combined with the beginning of the Soviet counter-offensive at Stalingrad, Allied success in the desert was seen to be a turning point in the war, marking the end of the German advance. Politically, this had two main consequences. First, it marked the end of any serious threat to Churchill's leadership; Cripps left the war cabinet for the Ministry of Aircraft Production where he saw out the rest of the conflict in relative obscurity. Second, as Allied forces gradually gained the ascendancy, minds turned more seriously to what would happen when victory was won; issues of post-war reconstruction and reform were now pushed to the top of the political agenda.

Beveridge and reconstruction

Churchill frequently insisted that Britain's only war aim was the defeat of the enemy. Labour, however, argued from the outset that the war could be used as a chance to reconstruct Britain's society and economy along more equitable and progressive lines. The party recognised that as the state mobilised its resources for a major war, socialist measures would be adopted as the government assumed wide-ranging powers over property and labour. As the government planned for war, so Labour argued it should simultaneously plan for peace. The conflict should be seen as an opportunity to sketch a blueprint for a new Britain: one in which government was prepared to intervene more actively in the lives of citizens to provide greater equality, opportunity and security; one which looked very different from the Britain which was scarred by depression and waste in the 1930s. When Labour entered the coalition in May 1940, Attlee demanded that the government demonstrate its commitment to positive war aims. The call was supported by the Ministry of Information, which argued that a vision of a new post-war Britain had to be offered to the country in order to maintain morale. Churchill remained unconvinced, but was prepared at least to concede the establishment of a War Aims Committee with no real powers in August 1940. The following January he made the token gesture of handing Arthur Greenwood ministerial responsibility for reconstruction questions. Greenwood's personal impact was minimal, but in June 1941 he appointed William Beveridge to chair what was intended to be a minor committee investigating social insurance benefits. Inadvertently, it was this decision which ensured that the coalition had to take seriously the issue of social and economic reconstruction.

Before the war Beveridge had built a reputation as an academic, broadcaster, newspaper columnist and public servant. With an ego to match his intellect he was initially disappointed with his post as chair of a minor interdepartmental committee. It was soon evident, however, that Beveridge intended to make the most of his position, compiling a report which proposed an overhaul of existing schemes of social insurance. This was to be his personal contribution to a new post-war Britain, a sense that was reinforced when the civil servants who worked alongside him refused to endorse publicly the far-reaching and contentious proposals contained in the final document. Beveridge's cultivation of press contacts ensured that when his report, *Social Insurance and Allied Services*, was published in December 1942, it was met with a blaze of publicity which in turn fed public enthusiasm and sales of the document. The most unlikely best-seller of the war, the Beveridge Report provided the plans for the architecture of Britain's modern system of social insurance; its other legacy was the way it exposed more completely the ideological fault lines which ran through the coalition.

Beveridge proposed a rationalisation of existing insurance schemes, based on the long-established principle of contributions from worker, employer and state. In return for a weekly flat-rate contribution from the employed, the state would provide comprehensive cradle-to-grave insurance: it was in essence a contract between state and citizens. The main difference between Beveridge's scheme and its predecessors was the principle of universality: all those employed would be compelled to contribute to the state scheme, all would be entitled to benefits regardless of need. Beveridge pushed his collectivist vision further by insisting that his scheme should be buttressed by full employment, family allowances and a national health service. The reasoning behind the scheme was conceptually flawed and ambiguous (Harris 1986: 246–9; Marquand 1988: 28–31), but opinion polls and surveys showed that the report had captured the public imagination. In 1943 the British Institute of Public Opinion recorded that 88 per cent of one sample supported implementation of the proposals: it was this level of public endorsement which forced the coalition partners to respond.

Previous wartime disputes between Conservative and Labour backbenchers had involved issues such as nationalisation, the abolition of the household means test, increases in old age pensions and coal rationing (Brooke 1992; 72–91). Compared with the battle over Beveridge, though, these were mere skirmishes. Labour members warmly approved of the report, not least because it was broadly in line with one of their own policy documents produced earlier in 1942. The report also had enormous symbolic importance for Labour as a test of the coalition's commitment to reconstruction (Brooke 1992: 147). The demand from the party's backbenches was for immediate legislation along the lines proposed by Beveridge, something with which the Liberals largely concurred. The reaction in Conservative ranks, however, was very different. According to a report which summarised backbench opinion, the Tories' first objection to the Beveridge scheme was on economic grounds; for them the post-war priority should be the revival of Britain's export trades rather than expensive social reform. The second complaint was based on principle; universal availability of benefits, they believed, would weaken individual incentives and fail to target assistance to those who were most in need (Cockett 1995: 61).

Aware that the ideological differences at issue could not be reconciled, coalition ministers played for time. From the day the report was published until parliament debated its recommendations in February 1943, the government steered a middle line between Labour commitment and Conservative caution. It welcomed the Beveridge scheme in principle, but refused to make any promises about spending or priorities. In the debate on Beveridge on 16–18 February, though, the limits of this compromise were exposed. Conservative speakers such as Sir John Anderson, the Lord President of the Council, and the Chancellor, Kingsley Wood, emphasised the financial implications of the Beveridge scheme and cautioned that no commitments could be made until the state of Britain's post-war finances became known. Herbert Morrison, the Labour Home Secretary, attempted to reassure his backbench colleagues that the government intended to work towards the goal of social reform, but it was too late to repair the damage caused by the negativity of Anderson and Wood. Following the lead of James Griffiths, Labour's own expert on social insurance, almost the whole of the Parliamentary Labour Party (PLP) outside the government defied ministers and supported an amendment which called for immediate action on Beveridge.

The total of 121 votes against the coalition was the largest anti-government vote of the war and for a while it appeared to threaten Labour's continued involvement in the administration. Labour backbenchers complained that their colleagues in office were failing to exert sufficient authority within the coalition and to deliver progress on issues such as post-war reconstruction: some raised questions about the benefits of remaining partners in a government dominated by Conservatives. Labour ministers responded with a defence of their position, reminding the party of the political dangers of breaking the coalition and allowing the Tories to appeal for a renewed mandate from the electorate at a time when Churchill was so popular in the country. As the logic of this argument was recognised and good relations within the party were restored, the longer-term advantages of the Beveridge episode for Labour started to become apparent. The revolt of the PLP showed observers that Labour was the main party committed to social reconstruction. Beveridge himself had commented after the parliamentary debate that the result of the post-war election, whenever it came, was already decided; the Tories would lose because of their lack of enthusiasm for his scheme. This claim says as much about Beveridge's self-importance as it does about wartime politics, but opinion poll data lent some support to his prediction. Although such data should be regarded with a degree of caution, the Gallup survey showed that Labour registered a steady lead in the polls from the beginning of 1943 until the election of 1945. The results of by-elections provided a similarly encouraging message for Labour. In four of the six by-elections held in the month of the Beveridge debate, the Tories' vote fell by 8 per cent; many of these votes appear to have been transferred to 'independent' candidates who endorsed Beveridge and whose wider political stance was barely distinguishable from mainstream Labour opinion. Jefferys was in no doubt about the importance of the Beveridge episode in the overall context of wartime politics. He argued that the first two months of 1943 represented the single decisive moment on the long road to 1945; more than anything else, the coolness of Conservative ministers towards the Beveridge Report had profoundly damaging consequences for the party (Jefferys 1991: 150).

The coalition partners' response to the Beveridge Report has been invested by historians with a significance that goes beyond Labour's victory in the post-war election. The wartime reaction to Beveridge is a crucial component of the wider historiographical debate about the existence or otherwise of a post-war political consensus. Proponents of the case for consensus argue that the post-war years were marked by a historically unusual degree of agreement between the main parties on several areas of policy: the most frequently cited are welfare reform, the maintenance of full employment, the operation of a mixed economy and conciliation of the trade unions. Those who adhere to this model of post-war British politics argue that the origins of consensus can be located in the war years. Addison (1975) provided the first scholarly attempt to sustain this proposition, arguing that as a result of co-operation in the coalition from 1940 onwards the main parties eventually arrived at a policy convergence. He accepted that there were some areas of policy on which agreement could not be reached – land ownership and nationalisation of industry were the most contentious – but these were outweighed by the range of issues on which there was little to choose between the coalition partners. Buttressed by changes in intellectual and popular opinion, he claimed, the three main parties went to the polls in 1945 committed to shared principles of social and economic reconstruction: the war had produced 'a massive new middle ground' in British politics (Addison 1975: 14). This analysis of the origins of the post-war consensus is broadly shared by a number of writers (Titmuss 1950; Barnett 1987; Kavanagh and Morris 1994; Lowe 1990; Dutton 1997b).

The argument that cross-party co-operation in wartime produced a consensus, though, has been challenged by several historians and political scientists (Harris 1986; Pimlott 1988; Jefferys 1991; Brooke 1992; Fielding, Thompson and Tiratsoo 1995). Critics of the consensus model argue that the coalition government was never more than a temporary expedient, held together by the pressure of war rather than by agreement over a range of policies. As the realisation of victory came closer and minds focused increasingly on the domestic issues involved in social and economic reconstruction, the political differences between the coalition partners became ever more apparent. At most the parties agreed about which problems would have to be addressed in the aftermath of war; they also agreed that certain problems could be solved; there was little common ground, though, about how they should be tackled, nor was there any agreement over priorities. A brief examination of the main issues which divide these competing interpretations of wartime politics illustrates the difficulty of constructing a convincing case for the existence of a consensus by 1945.

According to Addison, the first popular proclamation of the wartime consensus came in March 1943, when Churchill broadcast to the nation his vision of a post-war Britain that would be reconstructed under a four-year plan (Addison 1975: 227). The broadcast was typically Churchillian: heavy on rhetoric but light on specific commitments. Its purpose was to reassure listeners that the government was serious about social and economic reform, but away from the microphone the Prime Minister made no secret of his displeasure at being forced to address such issues at a time when final victory was nowhere in sight. In any case, the common issues of domestic politics failed to excite a statesman who was absorbed by the conflict on the world stage. His decision to appoint a Minister of Reconstruction in November 1943 did not signal a new interest in domestic reform, instead it should be seen primarily as a device for maintaining good relations with Labour. The brief of the new Minister, Lord Woolton, was to co-ordinate reconstruction plans from other departments rather than to initiate policy. This in part helps to explain why the coalition produced only two major pieces of reconstruction legislation: the 1944 Education Act and the 1945 Family Allowances Act.

Supporters of the consensus model cite these legislative achievements as evidence of the coalition's ability to reach agreement on detailed policy issues. It was only lack of time and the more immediate demands of the war effort, they claim, which prevented further acts from reaching the statute book before the coalition disbanded. On this analysis, the government's intention to make progress on reform was confirmed by the series of white papers it produced as a preliminary to drafting legislation. In 1944 white papers were published on employment policy, social insurance, a national health service and the control of land use. These were followed in March 1945 by a white paper on housing. According to Addison, in these documents the coalition laid the foundations of the National Health Service (NHS), acknowledged for the first time that the government had a responsibility to maintain a high and stable level of employment, and incorporated the main proposals of the Beveridge Report in a blueprint that was modified only slightly in the post-war Labour government's 1946 National Insurance Act. This was the legacy which the coalition apparently bequeathed to its successor. Lowe suggested that the reconstruction committees worked seriously, both at a political and administrative level, and achieved a considerable amount of bipartisan agreement (Lowe 1990:

159). However, he also acknowledged that the parties reached this agreement from distinctive ideological positions and that their shared perspectives covered only the medium-term objectives of a limited range of policies (Lowe 1990: 169).

Although such a qualified description of the terms and conditions of cross-party agreement by itself raises questions about the validity of the term 'consensus', some historians deny that even the level of agreement described by Lowe existed in wartime. The white papers produced by the coalition have been interpreted as substitutes for action rather than statements of legislative intent – as symbols only of the parties' shared identification of the post-war issues which had to be addressed. In each instance the publication of a white paper underlined the distance which separated the two main parties not only over the detail of policy, but over purpose, principles and priorities.

The discussion which surrounded the two-part white paper on social insurance, for example, showed that the parties disagreed about the principle of establishing a subsistence rate of benefit. Labour's commitment to a social security system which would provide a national minimum was not reflected in the document, leaving party spokesmen to promise that Labour would reintroduce this principle to government plans after victory in a post-war election (Brooke 1992: 187). On the shape of the future national health service, the two main parties struggled until the final hour to reach a compromise on the content of the 1944 white paper. The main points of disagreement were over the method of payment to doctors, the relationship between voluntary and local authority hospitals and the retention of private practice alongside the state scheme (Jefferys 1991: 130; Brooke 1992: 210). Labour emphasised that the white paper was a consultation document which would not tie the hands of a future administration. This determination to reject the compromise it had agreed as members of the coalition was later confirmed by the provisions of Labour's 1946 National Health Service Act (Morgan 1984: 152–63).

Perhaps the clearest example of a white paper which tried but failed to disguise ideological divisions within the coalition, though, was the 1944 document on employment policy. Although significant as the first official acknowledgement of the government's responsibility for maintaining high and stable levels of employment, the white paper contained mixed messages about the techniques and tools of economic management which would be used in pursuit of this aim. It conceded that there would be a greater degree of state intervention in the economy to regulate effective demand than had been the case hitherto, but it fudged several important issues: the extent to which budget deficits would be tolerated in order to finance higher public investment; the timing and scope of the relaxation of direct wartime economic controls; and the post-war balance between private and public enterprise. The omissions and ambiguities enabled each of the main parties to present the white paper as an endorsement of their own separate ideological positions. The Conservatives were able to interpret the document as confirmation of the primacy which would be afforded to the role of private enterprise, the defence of sterling and the revival of the export trades after the war. In contrast, Labour was able to claim that the pre-war orthodoxy of the Treasury, with its commitment to balanced budgets and a market-driven economy, had been replaced by a new commitment to state-directed economic management (MacLeod 1986: 86–9; Jefferys 1991: 170–4; Brooke 1992: 260–2; Cockett 1995: 63–5).

In each of the documents cited, the draftsmen had worked hard to produce proposals which barely satisfied Labour's minimum require-ments but which remained just inside the limits of what Conservatives were prepared to accept. It should be admitted at this point that a group of more progressive Conservatives – the Tory Reform Group – urged the party to reject economic liberalism and take a more positive line on social reconstruction. The work of this group, together with the suspension of the activities of the Conservative Research Department and the cancellation of several annual party conferences, makes it difficult to produce meaningful generalisations about agreed Tory positions on policy in wartime. Also, it is possible that Labour ministers sought to emphasise disagreements with Conservative counterparts over the white papers in order to reassure their own backbenchers and activists that life in the coalition had not blunted their radical edge. Even with these caveats, though, it is clear that the tensions exposed by the debate on social and economic reconstruction were serious. Certainly, the ideological differences were sufficient to call into question the existence of a wartime consensus; indeed, it was such differences between the parties which help to explain why the coalition did not survive beyond the end of the European war.

From the moment the wartime electoral truce was declared, Labour confirmed that no wider political truce existed and reassured their own supporters that the party reserved the right to resume electoral contests at any time. These reassurances, though, were not enough to persuade every party member of the benefits of co-operation with the Tories, even though joining the coalition was presented as nothing more than a temporary strategy for securing Labour's policy objectives in wartime. While the leadership recognised that membership of the coalition brought distinct political advantages – not least the public recognition which Labour ministers gained on the home front after May 1940 – the compromises and loss of independence which cross-party government entailed proved painful for many within the Labour movement. As the party's wartime reform programme was continually frustrated, the leadership found it ever more difficult to persuade colleagues that coalition was the best strategy. In February 1944 the ruling body of the party, the National Executive Committee (NEC), committed themselves only to support the coalition until the end of the war in Europe; later in September it was announced that Labour would contest the post-war election as a separate party and not as coalition partners. Although there were some within the party hierarchy who would have preferred to see the coalition extended beyond the conclusion of hostilities in Europe, their motives were driven more by tactical considerations of party advantage than optimism about the reform programme which a cross-party government might deliver. Any arrangement which delayed a contest between the two main parties appeared attractive to some, because of the fear that an election called in the immediate aftermath of victory would see Churchill's party swept back to power. This assumption was shared by most commentators, even though evidence was available at the time which pointed to an eventual Labour victory.

Popular attitudes and the 1945 election

Churchill's enormous popularity with the public was never in doubt during the war, but his personal standing did not necessarily translate into support for his party. A number of factors combined to deepen the unpopularity of the Tories in wartime and to deny the party victory in the post-war election. It has been argued that the Conservatives were rejected in 1945 because a sufficient number of voters remembered the unemployment of the 1930s and the broken promises of a Tory-dominated government after the first world war (Taylor 1965: 723). The fact that the Conservatives were held in some quarters to have mishandled the national interest in the pre-war and 'phoney war' periods has also been identified as a causal factor in their defeat: hence Harold Macmillan's claim that the 'ghost of Neville Chamberlain' cost the party the election of 1945. Addison shared this analysis and argued that the Tories were unlikely to win any general election after the evacuation of British forces from Dunkirk in June 1940 (Addison 1975:

162). By-election results also suggest that sustained military failures damaged the Conservatives rather than all partners equally in the coalition: the first victories of independent candidates against Conservatives occurred in spring 1942, after a sequence of Japanese successes against Britain in the Far East. The most serious political difficulties for the Tories, though, surfaced after the publication of the Beveridge Report. The party's lukewarm attitude to welfare reform contrasted sharply with the enthusiasm of Labour and it coincided with the development of a lead in the opinion polls which Labour retained for the remainder of the war. The Conservatives lost three by-elections between January 1944 and April 1945, despite the personal endorsement their candidates received from Churchill. In each case the victorious candidate had advocated full acceptance of the Beveridge recommendations; this implied that it was the failure of the Tories to produce credible and detailed plans for post-war reform after 1942 which made the shift in public opinion away from Conservatism unstoppable, culminating in the election defeat of 1945.

It would be a mistake to assume, though, that there is a law of electoral politics which delivers a Labour government each time there is public disenchantment with the Conservatives. The point about the post-war contest is that by 1945 Labour was ideally placed to take advantage of the Tories' declining political stock. In part this was the result of good fortune. Labour's years in opposition in the 1930s worked to the advantage of the party in the early phase of the war; they could not be criticised for British defeats and failures such as Norway and Dunkirk as they had not held power in the pre-war and 'phoney war' periods. But when Britain and its Allies began to secure victories, Labour naturally took a share of the credit as it had become a major partner in the coalition. The formation of a national government in May 1940 provided Labour frontbenchers with an opportunity to prove themselves in office without having to undertake the difficult task of first winning an election. Labour was known and trusted as a responsible party of government by 1945 despite its failure to win power since 1929. Labour also had the advantage of being able to distance itself from the coalition whenever it was under a cloud because Labour backbenchers formed the official opposition at Westminster. In this sense, the party led a useful double existence. Perhaps more importantly for Labour, the war helped to increase support for the party's policies of state intervention and economic collectivism. There is some debate about the level of popular commitment in this area, but there is broad agreement that the reorganisation of society and economy for 'total war' was at least a factor in the 1945 contest. As we have seen, Labour argued at the outset that the war should be used as a vehicle for social and economic reconstruction. In much the same way that the state mobilised its resources for war, so Labour claimed it should use its powers in the post-war world to promote economic efficiency, greater equality and social justice: the message was that the 'people's war' should be followed by the 'people's peace'. Labour's wartime agenda was adopted whole or in part by left-of-centre intellectuals, churchmen, journalists and officials in the Ministry of Information, all of whom recognised that the promise of a post-war 'New Jerusalem' played a valuable role in the maintenance of civilian morale. State responsibility for full employment, the provision of universal welfare benefits, the mobilisation of state powers to solve the housing shortage and a narrowing of the gap between rich and poor were policies which attracted increasing popular support in wartime. They were traditional Labour objectives and there was every reason for the electorate to expect by the time the campaign began in June 1945 that the party's commitment to progressive reform ran deeper than that of its main rivals.

The campaign proper, launched by Churchill with a radio broadcast on 4 June, was an ill-tempered and at times bitter contest; the main parties clearly welcomed the opportunity to fight each other in public after five years together in government. By common consent the Conservatives ran a poor campaign. It was dominated by Churchill and it lacked a positive central theme; instead it relied on a negative anti-Labour message, combined with a personal appeal to support the man who had led Britain to victory. The party's manifesto, written in the form of an address by Churchill, identified as priorities the continued war against Japan, the international post-war settlement, the demobilisation of the armed forces and the defence of traditional British freedom against domination by powerful state machinery. It was understandable that after years of immersing himself in global wartime strategy, Churchill should find domestic issues mundane and secondary, but his sense of priorities was at odds with a large proportion of the electorate who were mainly concerned with issues such as housing and employment. True, the manifesto did outline Conservative intentions to establish a framework of services which would meet the country's welfare requirements, but the party's wartime attitude towards reconstruction meant that such declarations lacked credibility. Also, it was difficult for the party to reconcile its commitment to an enhanced role for the state in the provision of welfare services with its frequently articulated fears about the development of an over-mighty state in post-war Britain.

Throughout the campaign the Tories proclaimed that state-led reform was an inappropriate way for Britain to adapt to the changed conditions of peace; instead, they argued for a return to free enterprise and a dismantling of wartime state powers as a pre-requisite to the restoration of the national wealth which had been lost during the conflict. The party's conviction that the dismantling of the wartime state apparatus was required was expressed most famously by Churchill at the start of the contest, when he warned that a Labour government committed to extensive state intervention would have to rely on 'some form of Gestapo' to enforce its authority. This rather awkward attempt to portray Labour as a party of extremists, inspired in part by Friedrich von Hayek's text *The Road to Serfdom* (1944), was repeated by a number of Conservative candidates. But as a strategy for raising fears about Labour's true intentions in office it was never likely to prove effective, if only because Labour ministers had served loyally under Churchill in the coalition. The other strategic error by the Tories was the decision to base the election campaign around their leader. Understandably, they predicted that voters would return Churchill to office in 1945 in recognition of his inspiring wartime leadership; unfortunately for the Tories, opinion polls and surveys produced by Mass-Observation suggested that while a large majority of the public had a high regard for Churchill as a war leader, only a minority regarded him as a suitable peacetime Prime Minister.

Labour's campaign in contrast was well organised and went largely to plan. Attlee's calm and perhaps rather dull character helped to reassure voters who were not natural Labour supporters that they could trust his party with power. He coped effectively with the controversial claim by Tories that real authority in the party resided with the chairman of the NEC, the left-wing Harold Laski, not with the leader of the party in parliament. He also refused to be drawn into a fight with Churchill over the 'Gestapo' speech, reacting calmly to the incident and ensuring that attention remained focused on his party's own policy agenda. The central theme of Labour's campaign was a positive one: in post-war Britain public welfare should take precedence over private interest. In line with this theme the manifesto emphasised those issues which polls suggested had most resonance with voters: housing, full employment and social security. The rhetoric deployed in the manifesto emphasised the practical rather than the ideological rationale behind Labour's proposals. For example, public ownership was justified as a strategy for increasing the efficiency of specific industries. The party's formal link with the trade unions was acknowledged, but it was presented as a relationship which would enable a Labour government to manage the economy with the consent of workers – even so, the party was careful to stress its identification with ordinary individuals and families rather than powerful vested interests. The national press generally agreed that Labour ran the more effective campaign. There is also evidence that Labour enjoyed unprecedented organisational advantages at both a national and constituency level over a Conservative party which had allowed its internal machinery to atrophy in wartime (Kandiah 1995: 25–30). And yet while opinion polls showed that Labour enjoyed a clear lead at the end of the campaign, most commentators predicted a Tory victory in 1945. The results announced on 26 July came as a surprise even to Labour's leaders.

Labour won 393 seats with almost 48 per cent of the votes cast – turnout was a little below 73 per cent. The Conservatives were reduced to 213 seats on approximately 40 per cent of the votes and the Liberals won 12 seats with a 9 per cent share. Labour formed its first majority administration with a lead of 146 seats over the other parties combined, the Conservatives suffered their worst defeat since 1906 and the Liberals were left to reflect on the inequity of an electoral system which consigned them to a narrow fringe of British politics despite securing a sizeable share of popular support. The distribution of seats confirmed as expected that the new government's core support was in Britain's large industrial cities; less predictable was its success in southern suburban England and rural areas such as Norfolk. Polls and surveys suggest that a majority of service personnel and younger voters supported Labour and that the party made significant gains among skilled workers and the lower middle class. The result is commonly described as a Labour landslide and the scale of the victory has been interpreted by some as evidence of a fundamental shift of popular political attitudes towards the left.

Ralph Miliband argued that the common experience of war radicalised the electorate, providing them with a new consciousness of their collective strength. This promoted a widespread desire for fundamental change, encouraged in part by admiration of the wartime performance of the Soviet Union and it was manifested in Labour's post-war electoral triumph (Miliband 1972: 272–85). Other historians agree that the 1945 result should be seen primarily as a victory for the Labour Party, even if they are not prepared to accept in full Miliband's thesis on the development of wartime political attitudes. In their view, a majority in the country desired change in 1945 and Labour was uniquely well placed to meet this demand (Addison 1975; Morgan 1984; Hennessy 1992).

However, it is important not to exaggerate the extent to which Labour's large majority in 1945 signalled a transformation in popular political attitudes. Despite their poor performance and a number of other disadvantages, the Conservatives managed to poll almost 10 million votes. When the turnout of voters is taken into consideration, it is notable that only one-third of the electorate voted Labour. Evidence suggests that only a minority of these Labour voters supported the party for ideological reasons. Most were not converted to socialism during the war; most were not interested in public ownership, industrial democracy or the nature of capitalist production. Instead, a majority simply believed that Labour was more likely to keep its promises to build houses, avoid mass unemployment and implement a social security scheme along the lines proposed by Beveridge. Labour reminded voters that the Conservatives had broken their promises of reform after the first world war. To make matters worse the Tories were also associated with the depression of the inter-war years, the apparent failure of appeasement and the defeats of 1940–2. Polls suggest that the war bred cynicism about politics and political parties; Labour's great advantage in 1945 was that it was less unpopular than the Conservatives (Mason and Thompson 1991; Fielding 1992; Fielding 1995; Fielding, Thompson and Tiratsoo 1995).

Conclusion

The beginning of the war coincided with the political rehabilitation of Churchill, who went on to become Prime Minister in 1940 after Lord Halifax turned down the chance to succeed Chamberlain. In contrast to the myth of Churchill as national saviour, the new Prime Minister took some time to establish his authority as head of the coalition government; he also had to manoeuvre skilfully to frustrate his critics until late 1942 – though he was helped in this regard by the shortage of credible challengers to his authority. Churchill was rather less sure footed after 1942 when reconstruction issues came to dominate political discussion; he failed to ensure that his party responded adequately to the widespread support for Beveridge and this failure contributed to the Conservatives' defeat in 1945. It has been argued here that the differences between the parties over social and economic policy were serious enough to call into question the thesis about the development of a wartime political consensus – it should be noted here that much of the post-war Labour government's reform programme was contested, both by political opponents and interest groups such as the British Medical Association and the Federation of British Industry. The absence of a wartime political consensus also helps to explain the bitterness displayed in the 1945 election campaign. It took the largest depression the industrial world has ever seen and war on an unprecedented scale to give Labour the chance to form its first majority government. This was the most important legacy of wartime politics. As shown, though, it would be a mistake to assume from this that a substantial proportion of the electorate had been radicalised by the experience of what came to be known as the 'people's war'.

Chapter 2

The people's war

The most powerful and enduring images of Britain in the second world war are associated with the home front: blitzed cities, communal air-raid shelters, the munitions factories of Britain's industrial heartlands and crowds of evacuees waiting for trains which would take them to the relative safety of the countryside. These are the most familiar symbols of the concept that became known as the 'people's war'. To an unprecedented degree the burden of war fell on the nation as a whole from September 1939, testing the resolve of the civilian population as much as the power of Britain's armed forces. The collective nature of the war effort was held to have produced profound social change: prewar divisions of class, wealth, status and power were allegedly set aside in favour of a new social cohesion which developed from the common experience of war and the shared aim of defeating the enemy. As the British faced the invasion scare of 1940, as the Luftwaffe attacked urban centres and as the nation prepared for the long hard struggle on the road to victory, rich and poor, male and female, majorities and minorities alike apparently submerged their differences and stood together in common defiance. The idea that the British developed a greater sense of collective consciousness in wartime which enabled them to make sacrifices, work together and abandon narrow self-interest in pursuit of a shared goal was continually promoted by government propaganda as a means of maintaining morale and heading off the danger of internal social conflict. The Ministry of Information and the BBC emphasised that the nation was fused together in a common cause and reassured the public that if they continued to work together, survival and eventual victory would be secured.

As well as functioning as a propaganda motif, though, the concept of a 'people's war' was also central to wartime debates on social reconstruction and the nature of the relationship between citizen and state. Social reformers in fields such as politics, academia and the church argued that the war encouraged Britons to identify with communal rather than individualistic values and that this in turn created an opportunity to construct a new social and political order on the basis of an enhanced role for the state in the lives of citizens. In the view of these reformers the demands of war produced an increase in state power and a growing acceptance of the legitimacy of state authority, both of which could be harnessed to the drive for government-led social change after the war. This change would not be confined to specific areas of social policy, instead it would involve the framing of a new social contract between state and citizen: one where the emphasis was on the idea of society as an organic body in which individuals shared public duties and rights, rather than on the idea of natural liberty and the inherently private rights and duties of individuals (Harris 1986: 235–7). The most obvious outward expressions of this new social contract were the institutions, apparatus and administrative arrangements of the post-war welfare state and managed economy.

The historiography on wartime social and economic themes has frequently endorsed all or part of the thesis that the war in Britain produced a heightened sense of public solidarity and idealism which in turn led directly to social change. Richard Titmuss, in an influential and often brilliant study of wartime social policy, argued that changed public values resulting from war helped to produce and legitimise the egalitarian social policies and collectivist economic measures adopted in part by the coalition and more fully by the post-war Labour government (Titmuss 1950). Angus Calder agreed that the war produced a radical groundswell in favour of social reform, but he went on to lament that these hopes were betrayed by a combination of capitalists, self-interested state bureaucrats and Labour ministers who possessed neither the ambition nor the political will to grasp the revolutionary moment (Calder 1992). Arthur Marwick rejected Titmuss's theory of the relationship between war and social change in favour of a more complex model, but he at least shared the view that the conflict led to profound changes in British society, caused in part by the collective nature of the war effort (Marwick 1968, 1974). The theme that the war altered public values and ushered in social change can also be found in general surveys of the period (Mowat 1955; Taylor 1965). More recent historiography, though, has raised serious doubts about the ways in which the conflict has been labelled a 'people's war' and about the validity of the war and social change thesis employed by Titmuss and others. The problem, in part, is one of measurement. Identifying outcomes in the form of legislative and institutional changes in the social sphere is a simple enough task. But tracing the precise origins of these changes and measuring their impact on millions of individuals over a long period of time is more problematic. More difficult still is the task of making meaningful generalisations about the attitudes, values and experiences of people in a highly complex, multi-dimensional and multi-layered society across six years of war. These are tasks, nevertheless, which historians continue to undertake.

Evacuation and the blitz

The first great social upheaval in Britain during the second world war was the evacuation of 'priority classes' and schoolchildren in September 1939. The movement of population from urban centres to safe, mainly rural, areas continued during the 'phoney war', despite the absence of German air-raids. By the end of the war approximately 4 million city dwellers had spent some time in the country – with the exception of direct experience of air-raids, evacuation was the crucial life-event for millions during the war, temporarily separating families while supplementing households in the host areas (Macnicol 1986: 7–8). According to the war and social change thesis, evacuation played a major role in the promotion of social solidarity as town met country and working class met middle class. The interaction of previously distant social groups was held to have increased national awareness of the problem of urban poverty, as reception halls across the country filled up with apparently malnourished and lice-ridden children, lacking adequate clothing and displaying little if any evidence of schooling. Stories about poverty-stricken evacuees filled the local and national press, speeches were made in parliament about the need to tackle the serious social problems highlighted by evacuation and the Prime Minister, Chamberlain, promised that remedial action would be taken. According to Titmuss, evacuation stirred the national conscience and produced important changes in social policy; these included the increased provision of milk and meals in schools, a more liberal attitude towards the means testing of benefits and the implementation of the 1944 Education Act (Titmuss 1950). In a recent article John Welshman provided some support for this thesis, arguing that the achievements of the School Medical Service were reassessed in the wake of evacuation as part of a more general change in attitudes to state welfare (Welshman 1998: 53).

However, this interpretation of the effect of evacuation requires some qualification. Reports from largely middle-class voluntary social work agencies identified working-class parental failure and 'problem families' as explanations for the poor condition of evacuees, not deep-seated social and economic deprivation. In their view a change in working-class mores rather than extensive social reform was required to correct the problems exposed by evacuation. Reports also discovered that many evacuee families found it difficult to reside with their hosts, to the extent that two families sharing the same home often lived almost completely separate existences, each family critical of the other. Middle-class hosts became increasingly reluctant to accommodate evacuees, while studies showed that evacuee families were usually most happy when they resided with hosts from a similar social background. In short, far from promoting cross-class co-operation and understanding, evacuation confirmed and often deepened class antagonism, in particular by reinforcing long-standing prejudices about the urban poor (Macnicol 1986: 27–8; Fielding, Thompson and Tiratsoo 1995: 21–3).

The relationship between evacuation and social reform which Titmuss and others have drawn is also problematic. It is clear, for example, that the provision of milk and meals was widely extended for schoolchildren in wartime. But plans to extend this provision had been drawn up in the 1930s regardless of the threat of war, while the relaxation of means-testing during wartime largely reflected the logistical problems of tracking those children who were entitled to free school milk as they moved across the country during evacuation (Macnicol 1986: 23–4). Similarly, the 1944 Education Act developed from pre-war plans – in this case the 1938 Spens Report – containing little that drew directly from wartime experiences or any conspicuous sense of social solidarity fostered by evacuation. In fact the 1944 Act, which introduced free secondary education using the tripartite model of grammar, technical and secondary modern schools, helped to entrench a socially divisive system which in the main benefited middle-class children (Thom 1986: 101–28).

German air-raids on British cities, which had been expected in the first weeks of war, began in earnest during September 1940. London suffered the heaviest raids, but other major towns and cities shared in the devastation. Interpretations of the British experience of the blitz on civilian centres are integral components of the 'people's war'. Popular images of the blitz emphasise that the crisis was met by shared defiance and common endeavour: communal shelters, frequently run by informal but elected committees; shops and businesses which refused to close despite the bomb damage; neighbours taking in homeless families; the volunteer wardens, fire-fighters and rescue workers scrambling through the rubble in search of survivors – these were seen as the outward expressions of the new communal and civic culture which developed among the urban population. For the first time the air-raids brought the reality of modern war directly to Britain's towns and cities. Even though a German invasion had been avoided, the battlefield now crossed civilians' homes and neighbourhoods.

There is no doubt that the blitz provoked countless acts of heroism, self-sacrifice and altruism. Also, urban Britain never suffered any lengthy period of social breakdown under the pressure of raids, continuing instead to meet the war effort's requirement for production, transport and administration. The problem with so many accounts of the blitz, however, is that they provide a monochrome picture of stoical resistance and social solidarity. Such accounts fail to acknowledge that the raids also drew understandable responses of a different kind, evidence of which can be found in Ministry of Information reports on civilian morale in 1940–1. A report on Coventry, for example, referred to 'great depression, a widespread feeling of impotence…and many open sign [sic] of hysteria'. In Portsmouth a report stated 'that looting and wanton destruction had reached alarming proportions. The police seem unable to exercise control' (Smith 1996: 97–8). In Bristol there was much talk of the people having been let down by the government, and of the possibility of a negotiated peace. In Plymouth a report conceded that morale among the local population had disappeared (Ponting 1990: 164).

Other evidence challenges the assumption that the raids helped to break down barriers of social isolation and class consciousness. Only a small minority of the population used communal shelters, for most individuals and families the blitz was a personal experience which in many cases probably heightened psychological individualism. Mass-Observation found that if the raids promoted wider social identification in any sense it occurred within specific localities rather than across the nation as a whole. The fact that certain districts suffered heavier and more frequent raids than others helped to produce a degree of class-based resentment, because it was working-class areas of high population density which suffered most and which often had the least adequate shelter provision. Home Intelligence also found that raids intensified the resentment which was directed at ethnic minorities. In particular, anti-Semitic attitudes, which were well established before 1939, increased in

London's East End and several other urban centres (Fielding, Thompson and Tiratsoo 1995: 25).

Rising crime rates further contradict the idea that a new communal culture developed in 1940. The aftermath of raids and the stretching of police resources provided opportunities for looting and property crime to become more widespread, the black market flourished and there was a marked increase in sexual crimes (Smithies 1982). Much of the increase in crime was a result of opportunist activity. Air-raid wardens and other officials were responsible for a good deal of the looting which followed bombing raids. Normally law-abiding citizens often responded to wartime privation by pilfering goods from work, drawing rations under false names and buying either forged or stolen ration coupons on the black market. In the disruption caused by war there were increased opportunities for white-collar crime: companies overcharged on government contracts, accounts were falsified and civil servants were bribed by people anxious to secure lucrative contracts. There was also an increase in violent crimes, such as robbery of shops and warehouses. In the press, the influx of servicemen from north America was often used to explain the rise in robbery, a practice which probably tells us more about the desire to preserve the British myth of the 'people's war' than it does about the causes of wartime crime. The murder rate showed a slight increase on average during the war years, but more noticeable was a sharp rise in the incidence of rape and other sexual offences. Wartime crime rates were comparatively low when set against the statistics of the post-war decades, but the fact remains that an increase in several categories of crime occurred after 1939.

Women at war

The theory that war promoted social change features frequently in studies of female roles in Britain since 1939. The mobilisation of women during the 'people's war', particularly after conscription of females was introduced in December 1941, led to a public re-examination of gender roles during wartime and a continued debate about the effect of the war on the status of women. Several writers have claimed that the war produced fundamental social and economic improvements for women, particularly in terms of their position within the labour market (Williams 1945; Goldsmith 1946; Titmuss 1958; Myrdal and Klein 1956; Marwick 1968, 1974). These views, however, have been challenged effectively by social historians and sociologists who argue that many of the changes which affected women during the war were often transitory or superficial. They also point out that sex-based inequalities persisted in the post-war period (Mitchell 1974; Smith 1981, 1984, 1986; Riley 1983; Summerfield 1984, 1988, 1993; Braybon and Summerfield 1987).

The early stages of the war offerred little evidence that the conflict would further the cause of female emancipation. Chamberlain's government made no determined attempt to mobilise female labour, despite pressure from women's groups such as the British Federation of Business and Professional Women who campaigned for women to be given greater opportunities to contribute to the wartime labour force. Instead, unemployment among women actually increased in the first few months of the war. The situation was only reversed after the new Minister of Labour read the reports of the Manpower Requirements Committee in 1940 and acknowledged that the employment of large numbers of women was vital. In 1941 Bevin persuaded government colleagues that the most effective way to secure this was through conscription. By 1943 the compulsory recruitment of females into the women's services, civil defence or munitions factories had helped to increase the number of women in the workforce by approximately 1,500,000 compared with 1939. Although in practice the National Service (No. 2) Act had the most immediate impact on single women aged between 19 and 30, the increased female presence in the labour force was due in part to the voluntary entry of married women into employment at a time when many husbands were in the armed forces and wives' earnings became vital. Whereas in 1931 only 16 per cent of working women were married, by 1943 the figure had climbed to 43 per cent, a rise that was helped by the provision of state-run nurseries for working mothers. Marwick used this increase and evidence from a business survey conducted at the end of the war to suggest that prejudice against the employment of married women was overcome during the war years (Marwick 1976).

Not only did women participate in the wartime labour force in greater numbers, the way in which they were distributed across occupations also changed. A major contribution to this process was made by the Extended Employment of Women Agreement of May 1940, brokered by Bevin and signed by the employers and trade unions in the engineering industry. The agreement meant that women could be employed in jobs previously reserved for male workers, but only for the duration of the war. This helped to increase the numbers of women employed in the traditionally 'male' sectors of industry; engineering saw the most significant rise, but transport, metals, chemicals and shipbuilding also witnessed changes. In contrast, the presence of women in traditionally 'female' and lower-paid sectors such as textiles, domestic service, food, drink and consumer services declined. In this way, it is claimed, the war contributed to the gender restructuring of the labour force and opened up new opportunities for women which enhanced both their earning power and self-esteem. It would be unwise, of course, to generalise about women's subjective responses to wartime employment – particularly in ways which failed to recognise important variables such as social class, age, ethnicity and marital status. But autobiographical evidence does suggest that many women viewed their wartime experience as an important phase of their personal development, enabling them to enjoy new opportunities and learn new skills (Braybon and Summerfield 1987).

Against this description of positive change for women in wartime, though, have to be set several important qualifications. Increased female participation in the workforce peaked in 1943 and declined thereafter; between 1943 and 1947 the number of women who left employment was approximately 1,750,000, so that by 1951 the proportion of all adult women in the paid labour force had largely returned to pre-war levels. This decrease can be explained to some extent by the unfavourable terms and conditions of work experienced by female employees. The long-established practice of sex differentiation in both public and private sector pay was continued in wartime and ensured that women received lower rates of pay than men engaged in equivalent work. Although some apparent progress was made towards the principle of equal pay in the engineering industry it only applied to the small minority of women who directly replaced men and were able to perform precisely the same job as their male predecessor without additional supervision. In practice, this part of the Extended Employment of Women Agreement was frequently circumvented by employers who either altered the work process slightly or ensured that female workers received some additional supervision in order to keep their wages below the male rate. The agreement also probably signalled the trade unions' determination to prevent male workers' wages from being undercut by cheap female labour rather than any commitment to equality between the sexes (Smith 1981). Average earnings for women industrial workers did increase during the war, but their rates of pay remained substantially below that of males.

In government and Whitehall the dominant view was that the issue of equal pay was best ignored, not least because any attempt to address it might provoke industrial unrest and conflict with the trade unions.

This stance eventually persuaded pressure groups such as the Woman Power Committee and the Joint Committee on Women in the Civil Service to establish the Equal Pay Campaign Committee at the beginning of 1944. In March their lobbying helped to produce a victory of sorts when an amendment to the 1944 Education Bill requiring equal pay for female teachers was passed against the wishes of the government by 117 to 116 votes. The victory, however, was shortlived. The vote in favour of equal pay was overturned when the coalition government – which had suffered its first parliamentary defeat of the war – insisted that it would resign unless the amendment was defeated in a second Commons vote. To avoid any repetition of the controversy, the government effectively removed equal pay from the wartime political agenda with the appointment of a royal commission on the issue. No further consideration would be given to equal pay until the commission reported; when this eventually happened in 1946 no policy recommendations were offered, the changed political context made equal pay less of a pressing issue and the post-war Labour government largely ignored the main findings of the commission. In short, despite the fact that women had been coerced into the wartime labour force, borne the hardships and performed well, successive governments ensured that sex differentiation in pay remained in place during and after the war (Smith 1981).

Inequality in pay was one of several manifestations of wartime sexual discrimination. Another in the first half of the war concerned the rates of compensation paid under the 1939 Personal Injuries (Emergency Provisions) Act, which meant that civilian women with war injuries were paid lower rates of compensation than men. This practice was condemned by politicians across the political divide, but ministers argued pragmatically that a concession of the principle of equal compensation would increase pressure for government to concede the wider principle of equal pay. After the strength of feeling among MPs on the issue became known in 1942, though, a select committee was appointed which eventually reported in favour of equal compensation for war injuries. The government announced its acceptance of this principle in April 1943 (Smith 1981: 663). It was an important victory for women's groups, but it was a relatively isolated one achieved after a hard fought battle more than three years into the war. As such it is an instructive example of the scale of the challenge facing women who attempted to change the culture of sexual discrimination which remained in Britain even during the 'people's war'.

The need to mobilise women for the war effort conflicted with long-standing assumptions about female roles in society. This conflict presented the wartime government with a dilemma: on one side it needed to recruit sufficient female labour to meet production targets; on the other, it was anxious to maintain a traditional stance on the sanctity of the home and the mother's place within the family (Summerfield 1993: 66). One consequence of the latter concern was that women with particular domestic 'duties' were exempt from conscription. For example, mothers living with a child who was under 14 were not eligibile for call up, married women could not be conscripted into the armed forces and childless servicemen's wives could not be sent away into war work. Women who were called up for service usually found that paid employment was an addition to their domestic responsibilities of running a household, not a replacement. This 'double burden' was made particularly onerous by rationing, shortages, air-raids and other wartime disruptions. The way in which women performed a dual role in wartime led some commentators to conclude that the war pointed a way forward for married women: showing how it was possible to engage in paid work without causing any detrimental effects to home and family life (Myrdal and Klein 1956). But a more significant point is that domestic work continued to be seen as the responsibility of females even after women were conscripted into the labour force.

The government's wish to recruit female labour while at the same time minimising any challenge to sexual stereotypes was evident in its propaganda drive. Ministry of Information short films such as *Jane Brown Changes Her Job* and *Night Shift* emphasised that women could take on manual occupations without sacrificing their femininity (Carruthers 1990: 240). Editors of women's magazines were invited to serve on a government committee which helped to ensure that particular messages were conveyed to women about issues such as dress and appearance. Women's magazines carried a recurrent theme of 'beauty as duty', encouraging readers to beautify themselves in order to maintain men's morale. To assist this process supplies of rubber and steel were set aside by the Board of Trade to make corsets, a fashion firm was commissioned to produce the regulation corset for female service personnel, women munitions workers were given special allowances of high-grade face make-up, and hairdressers were allowed to prevent key staff from being transferred to essential war industries (Kirkham 1995: 14–15). All of this contributed to the idea that women's war work was special and in some ways unnatural, a short-term expedient which required specific arrangements to be made so that women could adjust to their new environment in a way that preserved their essential feminine qualities. Women's magazines also continued to promote the view that the home and family were women's primary responsibility, a message which implied that paid employment for many women should be no more than a temporary wartime adjustment.

Indeed, social policy during and after the war suggests that the government wished to encourage women to see themselves primarily as full-time housewives and mothers. The major political parties did not disassociate themselves from the views expressed in the Beveridge Report, which aimed to promote women's acceptance of traditional sex roles, ensuring that as mothers they helped to renew Britain's population. It was partly in response to concerns about the birth rate that a Family Allowances Act was passed in 1945, though the extent to which this affected decisions on family size is debatable. The withdrawal of hundreds of state-run nurseries at the end of the war restricted the opportunities for mothers with young children to take paid employment, despite forecasts of a severe post-war labour shortage. More influential than these forecasts was psychological research which pointed to the need for mothers with children aged under two to stay at home rather than work. In addition, the reluctance of many employers to offer part-time working arrangements meant that mothers of school-age children frequently experienced problems finding paid work. This helps to explain why the greatest increase in female employment after the war was among women aged over 35. It was these who were targeted by the Attlee government's propaganda, which aimed to persuade women to re-enter the workforce at a time of pressing labour shortages from late 1946 onwards. Mothers with young children were specifically excluded from the recruitment drive on the grounds that their first duty was to home and family (Carruthers 1990: 248–9).

Prior to the outbreak of war a marriage bar affected most public and many private sector occupations, which meant that women were forced to resign from their jobs once they were married. The regulation was suspended during the war because of labour shortages and the government eventually abolished the marriage bar for teachers and civil servants, motivated again it seems by the need to overcome recruitment shortages rather than principle. The Royal Commission on Equal Pay and the Whitley Council Report on Marriage Bars, both produced in 1946, further dismantled statutory discrimination against women in the labour force. However, several major firms surveyed in the same year as these reports were published indicated their intention to restore the marriage bar, casting doubt on claims that the war helped to promote more positive attitudes towards the employment of married women. In fact, in many institutions the barriers against the employment of married women were not formally removed until the 1950s.

Barriers which restricted employment opportunities for married women were given added significance by the post-war increase in the marriage rate. The figures for England and Wales show a surge in the marriage rate in 1939 and 1940 to 22.5 per thousand. The rate then fell sharply to 14.0 in 1943, but climbed again from 1945 to 1948 to rates above 18.0 per thousand in what has been described as a post-war marriage boom (Winter 1986: 152–3). Not surprisingly, the rise in marriage rates was accompanied by a climb in the birth rate, temporarily reversing a decline which had continued since the 1870s. In 1941 the birth rate at 13.9 per thousand was the lowest official figure ever recorded; but it climbed thereafter to a post-war peak of 20.6 per thousand in 1947 (Smith 1986: 220). These increases could be interpreted as confirmation of the fact that the war years had neither encouraged nor empowered women to break free from their traditional domestic roles. But the data should also be set in a context which recognises that changes affecting gender roles within marriage were being reported at the time. So, for example, while the marriage rate was higher in 1947 than in 1938, it was possible that women's expectations about marriage also changed between these two dates. The Royal Commission on Population established in 1945 made reference in its report to the 'companionate' marriage, in which partners had more equality of status. The war was held to have accelerated the trend towards the companionate marriage, even though husbands continued to be regarded as the family's principal wage earner in most cases. Although many young single women left employment after the war, the self-esteem and sense of independence they developed in the wartime workforce or services was believed to have made them much less likely to accept a subordinate role within marriage in the post-war years. There are several factors which contributed to the sharp rise in the divorce rate after 1945, but part of the explanation could be that women developed higher expectations of marriage in the post-war world and greater self-confidence to break a marriage which was not meeting these expectations. Research in the 1950s suggested that the companionate marriage was an ideal rather than reality for most women, but it was significant none the less that a new marital objective had been more widely established. This is one example of the changes which affected women of different ages, classes and ethnic groups during and after the conflict, creating new expectations and social norms (Summerfield 1993: 78). It would be a mistake to argue that there was a transformation of women's socio-economic status as a result of the war, but it would be equally misleading to claim that the war produced no longer-term consequences at all for women in any field.

Civil liberties, citizenship and the state

Conscription of adult males and females was one of the most striking illustrations of the extension of state powers in Britain during the second world war. By 1941 increased state interference in the nation's social and economic life had made Britain the most rigorously planned and regimented society in Europe (Cockett 1995: 58). To an extent, therefore, the collective nature of the 'people's war' was imposed on the British top-down by the authority and power of the state. The main legislative basis of this increased authority was the Emergency Powers (Defence) Act of May 1940, which gave the state sweeping powers to do whatever it believed was necessary for the war effort. Internal security requirements and the material demands of war obviously meant an enhanced role for the state, but it should be acknowledged none the less that an immediate corollary of this was an erosion of civil liberties. Much of the literature on the wartime home front fails to engage seriously with this aspect of policy, but at least one major work argues that the government's handling of activities which infringed personal freedom was questionable (Stammers 1983).

In certain areas the extension of state power drew on precedents from the first world war and was relatively uncontentious. For example, one lesson of the earlier conflict was that conscription should be introduced at the beginning of a major war rather than the middle. As a result, the legislation which enabled the government to prepare for full military conscription of men was passed in the summer of 1939 and was succeeded by a National Service Act in September. The small proportion of males who registered as conscientious objectors signified the extent to which military conscription was regarded as legitimate: in late 1939 it was about 2 per cent and by the summer of 1940 it was down to 0.5 per cent (Pelling 1970: 249). These figures were recorded in spite of the fact that conscientious objection was now accepted on grounds other than religious – a direct contrast to previous practice. In May 1940 conscription was extended to the industrial workforce, a decision that was justified by the government on the grounds that they required umbrella powers over all persons; it was now possible for the state to direct anyone in the United Kingdom to work anywhere or perform any service required in any place. By spring 1941 the operation of conscription and other industrial controls had been refined to a point where the Minister of Labour had extensive powers over labour mobility, worker discipline, conditions, hours and wages. Ernest Bevin preferred to rely on voluntarism and free collective bargaining where possible, but where necessary he did not shrink from using a range of coercive powers over the labour force which had never before been available to a British minister.

Similarly widespread powers were taken by the state to monitor and restrict the flow of information. There was no question that the government had a duty to prevent the leakage of information to the enemy which might be of military value. The problem lay in interpreting this duty and defining the circumstances in which censorship could be justified, not least because of the way in which Britain's war effort came to be portrayed as a defence of democratic values against totalitarianism. Government controls over the press are relevant here but are discussed in more detail elsewhere (Chapter 4). These controls were accompanied from 1 September 1939 by censorship of postal and telegraphic communication, a process which involved a network of censorship offices across the country and the employment of over 10,000 civil servants. External censorship covered material which was sent out of the country, including letters, telegrams, books and news agency reports. The primary objective was to prevent information of military value from reaching the enemy, but the government also stated its intention to restrict the circulation of material which brought into disrepute the Allied war effort. Internal censorship covered the flow of information within Britain and does not appear to have been used in any systematic way before the invasion scare of May 1940. But in June the Home Secretary signed a general warrant which enabled the authorities to censor internal mail and to make snap checks on telegrams and telephone calls. Stammers was unable to assess the extent to which internal censorship was imposed because the relevant material in the Public Record Office was not available. But he argued nevertheless that the state probably used its powers to monitor British communists, Trotskyists and other dissidents who were critical of government policy (Stammers 1983: 137).

More direct action to counter threats to internal security was taken in May 1940 with the introduction of internment – this allowed for indefinite detention of suspected subversives without trial. Oswald Mosley and other members of the British Union of Fascists were among the first to be arrested and interned; Mosley remained in detention until November 1943 when he was released controversially on grounds of ill health. The Northern Ireland government, with the full support of Westminster, also interned a number of known activists in the Irish Republican Army, a policy that was mirrored in the Irish Free State. For the most part, detentions such as these were highly selective and relatively easy to justify. It should also be remembered in this context that members of the Independent Labour Party, Trotskyite factions and British communists, most of whom at one time or another opposed Britain's involvement in the war, were not interned (Calder 1992: 133). More controversial, though, was the decision to intern about 27,000 German, Austrian and Italian nationals between the summers of 1940 and 1941, despite the fact that many of them had been resident in Britain for a number of years, obeyed the laws of the state, paid taxes to the exchequer and contributed to the nation's economic, social and cultural life.

The main preparatory work for the policy of internment began in October 1939 when Tribunals across the country were given the task of classifying Germans and Austrians who were resident in Britain. There were three categories of 'enemy alien', ranked according to security risk: category A aliens were to be interned; category B were to have their freedom of movement restricted; and category C were to be exempt from restrictions as they were not considered a threat. Out of an approximate total of 74,000 individuals examined, only 600 were recommended for internment while 64,000 were placed in category C – about 56,000 of these were accepted as genuine refugees who had fled Nazi persecution. However, despite the fact that such a large number of these foreign nationals had passed security checks both before and during the war, the government decided to introduce a policy of widespread internment in May 1940. In part this reflected the security concerns of Britain's military chiefs following Hitler's attack on the west. But it also followed a campaign in newspapers such as the *Daily Mail* and *The Times* calling for the detention of enemy aliens. On 12 May a wide coastal belt stretching from Inverness to the eastern edge of Dorset was declared 'protected' and all German males aged 16–60 within this belt were rounded up for 'temporary' internment. On 16 May all German and Austrian males in category B across the country were rounded up, to be joined within days by thousands of females. By June chief constables had been ordered to extend internment to all male category C aliens under 70, with the exception of individuals such as key workers and the disabled who were exempted (Lafitte 1988: 70–3).

Within two weeks of Italy's entry to the war on 10 June about 4,500 Italians had been rounded up and interned.

According to Lafitte, the conditions in which internees were held failed to meet the minimum standards laid down by the Prisoners of War Convention. The problem here was that most internees were not technically regarded as prisoners of war, so there was no neutral protecting power to act on their behalf, nor – unlike military prisoners of war – were their British counterparts in Germany whose reciprocal treatment would have to be considered by the authorities (Lafitte 1988: 93). Camps such as those at Bury, Huyton, Kempton Park racecourse and the Isle of Man were overcrowded, deficient in supplies and amenities and in the worst cases damp and rat-infested. Despite the fact that internees were separated from their families at very short notice and held in camps which were dispersed across the country, no systematic records were kept of the movement of individuals and the authorities delayed setting up any effective channel of communication between the camps and the outside world. The exchange of postal communication was slow and erratic and for some time internees were barred from possessing books, newspapers or radios. Within the camps Nazi sympathisers were held alongside prominent anti-Nazis and German Jews, some of whom had spent years in Hitler's concentration camps before escaping to Britain. These refugees who had experienced persecution by the Nazis had more reason to fear a German invasion of the home islands than most Britons. Yet they were held as security risks and in a few cases the anxiety caused by detention led internees to commit suicide.

Internment was intended to be a prelude to deportation. In the first half of July 1940 almost 8,000 internees were shipped to Canada and Australia. Bureaucratic failure meant that those who were deported were frequently unaware of their intended destination, nor were they allowed to contact their families before being removed from the country. Strong criticism of this policy began after the *Arandora Star*, bound for Canada, was sunk by a German U-boat on 2 July with the loss of about 175 Germans and almost 500 Italians. Although early official reports claimed that the ship contained only known fascists, it soon emerged that a number of those drowned were former refugees. As more details became known about the policies of internment and deportation, pressure mounted on the government to modify its handling of the aliens issue. White papers on internment were issued by the government in July and August and in the latter month the release of internees began. As fears of an imminent German invasion receded, the number of releases increased; by the middle of February 1941 over 10,000 internees were free and by July 1942 only a hard core of about 400 known Nazi sympathisers remained in the camps.

Britain of course was not the only country which interned civilians during the second world war. There was also a precedent for the policy in Britain from 1914 to 1918 and it was possible to justify the employment of some form of detention without trial of foreign nationals on security grounds in the crisis months of 1940. But it is hard to disagree with Holmes's view that internment was insensitive, badly handled and inefficiently organised. He also argues persuasively that the policy should not be viewed as an irrational episode, an unfortunate product of the extreme pressure of war. Instead, it developed out of the hostility towards alien refugees which existed in Britain long before 1939 and which was reinforced rather than eroded during the 'people's war' (Holmes 1988: 191–2). It also reflected the increased power of a state engaged in total war.

The infringement of civil liberties confirmed the extent to which the wartime state was able to impose its will on citizens. However, contemporary observers and subsequent commentators have argued that the extension of state powers during the conflict had more profound and benevolent consequences than the temporary curtailment of individual freedoms. The collective experience of war and the apparent ability of the state to mobilise the national resources for a common goal were believed to have paved the way for a new relationship between citizen and state. This relationship grew out of the tacit wartime contract between government and people: in return for the civilian population's tolerance of compulsory measures in pursuit of victory, the government committed itself to the fight against material and social deprivation beyond the end of the conflict. The clearest expressions of the new relationship were to be found in the Beveridge Report and post-war welfare state, the central purpose of which was the provision of a wide range of social and economic services to all citizens.

The idea that the state should retain an enhanced role in the economic and social lives of citizens in peacetime did not win unanimous approval. Opposition in particular came from economic liberals in groups such as the Progress Trust, the National League for Freedom and the Society of Individualists, all of whom drew intellectual sustenance from the warnings of F. A. Hayek about the connection between state planning and the rise of corruption, tyranny and totalitarianism (Cockett 1995: 57–99). In the unique circumstances of war, however, the momentum was with those reformers who wished to harness the power of the state in the construction of a new social and political order, based on a degree of state intervention and centralisation of services which would have been unacceptable before 1940. These reformers were a diverse collection, ranging from William Beveridge, John Maynard Keynes, Archbishop William Temple, J. B. Priestley and George Orwell, to the Labour Party, the Common Wealth Party and the Tory Reform Group. Their agenda was made more palatable for 'middle opinion' by the publication of a special issue of *Picture Post* in January 1941, entitled 'A Plan for Britain' (Finlayson 1994: 255). Reformers also found important allies for the cause in those state agencies whose task was to convince civilians and soldiers alike that the war effort was worth the sacrifices demanded. Both the Ministry of Information and the Army Bureau of Current Affairs emphasised concepts such as fairness, decency, trust and reciprocity in their discussions of the values that would characterise post-war British society (Morgan and Evans 1993: 61).

The main blueprint which explained how the state could begin to achieve the outcomes desired by reformers was provided by Beveridge in 1942. The revolutionary principle that was contained in his report was universality – the provision of insurance by the state to all individuals, protecting them at every stage of the life cycle from inadvertent loss of income and guaranteeing them an agreed minimum standard of living. According to T. H. Marshall, Beveridge devoted little space to the defence of the principle of universality because it had become so obvious that the mutual service society of the war should become the mutual benefit society of the peace. Nevertheless, he continued, it was important not to lose sight of the fact that universality expressed a spirit that was definitely new (Marshall 1963: 279). The principle was significant because it altered the superstructure of legitimate expectations which citizens had of the state – for Marshall, these expectations were of more direct concern to individuals than legally enforceable rights (Marshall 1950: 58). In short, the war led citizens to expect a better range and quality of services from the state than ever before.

Richard Titmuss agreed that the reduction of inequalities and a flattened pyramid of social stratification were positive consequences of mass mobilisation (Titmuss 1958: 86). But he was critical of the terms and conditions of the relationship between citizen and state as set out in the Beveridge Report and the subsequent 1946 National Insurance Act. As Jose Harris has explained more fully in several works, the Beveridge scheme of social security was based on a contract between individuals and the state. Most of the finance was to be provided by the system's members and employers, with the state covering only one-sixth of most insurance benefits. In other words, despite the emphasis on universalism it was the payment of regular contributions to the state scheme which entitled individuals to benefits, not their status as citizens or members of a national community (Harris 1977, 1986, 1996). Self-help was placed at the centre of the new welfare state. Indeed, to qualify for the full entitlements of citizenship, individuals were obliged to find employment and contribute national insurance payments – most married women qualified via an employed husband. Furthermore, to achieve the twinned goals of full employment and universal welfare provision, Beveridge expected citizens to accept coercive measures from the state: compulsory training schemes for the unemployed, centralised direction of labour and extensive public control over investment, prices and incomes (Harris 1986: 248).

At its critical point, therefore, the relationship between citizen and state after the 'people's war' was defined in rather narrow, prosaic terms. The institutions and arrangements of the post-war welfare state, combined with the commitment to full employment, meant that British society after 1945 was different in key respects from the society of the inter-war years. But British citizenship was not reconstructed in any fundamental way as a result of the conflict. Wartime surveys found that while a majority desired improved welfare provision, there was widespread reluctance among the public to engage in the debate on reconstruction. Many of those questioned replied that they wanted post-war change, but they were unable to offer any specific ideas about what such change should involve (Mason and Thompson 1991: 58). There was a good deal of cynicism in the country about the state's ability to deliver on the promise of a brave new world. And in the latter years of the war surveys found widespread indifference or hostility to the idea of fundamental social reconstruction (Harris 1994: 244). The reasons for this were captured well by wartime research on attitudes to housing. The findings showed strong preferences for a return where possible to the normalcy and privacy of pre-war home life: no more sharing or billeting; houses instead of flats; the home as a retreat from the outside world rather than a unit within a wider community (Fielding, Thompson and Tiratsoo 1995: 33–9). In short, by the end of the war citizens focused overwhelmingly on their own needs and those of their families rather than identifying in any strong sense with the state, nation or community.

Conclusion

It was a people's war in as much as Britain mobilised its population for war to a greater degree than any other nation – taking account of the intensity and duration of mobilisation. This population overwhelmingly supported the national effort: even allowing for the impact of propaganda, the absence of a strong peace movement or large-scale anti-war demonstrations is striking. At a very general level the state ensured that a truly national campaign was fought: conscription, rationing, requisitioning and taxation cut across some traditional social boundaries and produced a degree of social levelling. In the course of this campaign millions of Britons displayed altruism, courage and a willingness to make sacrifices – those born after 1945 should never lose sight of this feature of the war effort. Nevertheless, half a century after the conflict there is a similar requirement for historians to acknowledge a more complex and nuanced picture of the wartime home front than the one contained in traditional versions of the 'good' war: one which includes the looting and hysteria in the aftermath of air-raids, rising crime rates, hostile reactions to ethnic minorities, infringements of civil liberties and class-based resentment. It is also important that in the search for general trends and the national picture, the complexity and diversity of society and the way in which the war progressed through distinct phases across its six years are not overlooked.

The main features of the political dimension of the people's war have been overdrawn. True, there was some public discussion of reconstruction issues, particularly in the wake of Beveridge. Also, the state's activities and areas of responsibility increased during the war. At the end of the conflict there was an ill-defined sense that the state should continue to do more for British citizens – particularly among those, such as the homeless, who had most to gain from improved public services. Moreover, Labour's landslide victory in 1945 appeared to signal that political values had changed in some fundamental way. Against this, however, it should be recognised that in many cases developments in public policy drew on pre-war origins, they did not arise spontaneously from the conflict. Far from generating consensus the reconstruction agenda was contested at almost every point, by interest groups as well as political parties. The insurance principle at the heart of the new welfare state signalled that there was no transformation of the relationship between citizen and state as a result of war. And despite the rhetoric of equality which accompanied the people's war, it was to be some time before important aspects of discrimination were tackled in Britain. The colour bar remained legal until the 1960s, even though in practice its operation varied across the country. Women, meanwhile, had to wait until the 1970s before the principle of equal pay between the sexes was established in law. The restructuring of the wartime labour force undoubtedly had positive results for many women in both the public and private spheres, but the dismantling of the wartime economy saw a significant shift towards pre-war norms in gender relations. In short, the benefits of the people's war bypassed large numbers of its participants.

Chapter 3

The wartime economy

War tested Britain's ability to mobilise its economic resources for a long, draining and expensive national effort. The Emergency Powers (Defence) Act of August 1939 was the first in a series of measures which enabled the government to intervene in the economy on an unprecedented scale. As the war progressed an extensive network of economic controls was established, covering almost every aspect of supply, production and trade. The machinery of government was redesigned to administer these controls (Hancock and Gowing 1949; Chester 1951) and some fifty economists were recruited into Whitehall to act as advisers (Cairncross 1995: 20). In the 'phoney war' there had been some reluctance to exploit these powers to the full: Chamberlain's government was ideologically opposed to extensive state intervention in the economy; it feared that a rapid mobilisation of resources for war production would have damaging economic consequences, and mutual suspicion between government and trade unions meant that imaginative manpower policies were rejected as unlikely to work. Therefore, although there was some departure from pre-war orthodoxy before May 1940, the most significant developments in the mobilisation of the war economy came after Hitler's attack on the west and the setting up of Churchill's wartime coalition. This chapter will assess the main measures used to gear the economy for war, the performance of Britain's wartime economic effort and the legacy of the conflict for the post-war economy.

Organising the war economy

The coalition government had a more active approach to the planned use of physical resources than its predecessor. The most important of these resources was manpower, control of which was the responsibility of the coalition's Minister of Labour and National Service, Ernest Bevin. His task was to distribute labour between competing needs: to balance the demands of the armed forces, the requirements of war production and the needs of civilian industry and services. By the end of 1942 the principle of manpower budgeting had been formalised and the Ministry of Labour and National Service was recognised as the most important wartime department of state. In theory Bevin had massive powers over labour from the outset: Regulation 58A of the new Emergency Powers (Defence) Act of May 1940 gave him the authority to require individuals to register for war work and then to direct them to work under terms and conditions laid down by the Ministry. These regulations were extended over time and by the middle of the war all adults up to the age of 50 had been registered. At the peak of labour mobilisation approximately 10 million persons were either in active service or employed in the munitions industries. Also, some 8 million employees were affected by Essential Work Orders, which had been introduced in 1941 to keep workers in place in jobs which were vital to the war effort – for example, in engineering, coal, shipbuilding, iron and steel – by restricting the rights of employees to resign from a job and the rights of employers to dismiss workers (Aldcroft 1986: 166). In practice, however, Bevin relied as far as possible on the voluntary principle, partly because of his background in the trade union movement, but also to avoid a repeat of the industrial unrest which broke out in the first world war. He consulted both the TUC and employers' federations over policy and used his powers to direct labour sparingly. In fact, only some 250,000 men and 90,000 women were directed into wartime industrial work which they had not chosen (Middlemas 1986: 31).

Bevin's desire to win consent from all sides was reflected in the formal arrangements he made for consultation. The main agreements about labour matters were reached on the Joint Consultative Committee, a body with equal representation of management and unions, whose twice monthly meetings were usually chaired by Bevin (Middlemas 1986: 21). The inclusion of the trade unions in an official framework signalled an important change from the time when relations between government and the TUC were at a low point under Chamberlain. It recognised that the support of the unions was vital if labour was to be transferred from civilian production to essential war industries without widespread unrest. Co-operation from the unions was also vital in the constant battle against skills shortages. As well as ensuring that manpower levels were adequate in each industry, the

Ministry of Labour also had to ensure that workers had the skills required to produce good quality material for the war effort. This meant that key workers had to be prevented from joining the armed forces and accelerated training programmes had to be set up for new workers. More controversially, though, it meant that complex jobs had to be redesigned in ways that made them suitable for unskilled or semi-skilled workers. This process, known as dilution, usually involved dividing work into a set of less complex tasks and often made use of new machinery. The trade unions were never entirely comfortable with dilution as they feared that it would undermine the value of skilled labour in the post-war world, but they were prepared to compromise with government and employers for the sake of the war effort. The unions' acceptance of dilution became of vital importance when millions of women entered the labour force after 1941, particularly in the engineering industry which suffered some of the most severe shortages of skilled labour.

The need to maintain good relations with the unions helps to explain why Bevin was reluctant to impose statutory wage controls, preferring instead to let free collective bargaining continue. In his view, workers who were on the receiving end of labour controls were entitled to good working conditions and welfare arrangements and the right to negotiate through their trade union for adequate wages (Booth 1989: 46). Although technically strikes and lockouts were outlawed by Order 1305 of July 1940, workers continued to use stoppages as a bargaining counter with employers – in fact, short strikes were often regarded by the state as a useful way for hard-pressed workers to let off steam, so penal sanctions were rarely applied.

Manpower controls were an important tool in the government's direction of war production. As the supply needs of the military increased, the state organised the expansion of the munitions industries and the consequent contraction of civilian production. In addition to the transfer of labour into essential war industries, controls over the allocation of raw materials, prices, building and investment were used by the government to channel resources into military production. A Production Executive was established to oversee the use of resources and once again Bevin ensured that unions and management were consulted over policy – this time in the National Production Advisory Committee for Industry (Middlemas 1986: 21). In an attempt to increase productivity, Joint Production Committees were used to channel ideas about efficiency and new methods from the shopfloor to management – it should be recognised, though, that responsibility for meeting central production targets remained with management throughout the war.

The state's direction of war production was strengthened by its position as the largest buyer of supplies for the war machine. The Ministry of Supply met the needs of the army, the new Ministry of Aircraft Production supplied the RAF from May 1940 and the Admiralty retained control over the navy's supply requirements. The Ministries of Supply and Aircraft Production soon took responsibility in effect for most manufacturing industry, investing in new capacity on a massive scale in order to increase production (Edgerton 1992: 92–3). In contrast, the Board of Trade had to manage a reduction in the output of civilian goods. As a result there were major changes in the economy's product mix during wartime: the production of consumer goods probably fell to no more than half its pre-war level, leading to shortages of many household goods such as furniture and clothing (Aldcroft 1986: 173, 180).

Directing the change from civilian to war production was made easier for the state by the large amount of industrial raw materials which were imported into Britain: these could be controlled at the ports and then issued to manufacturers under government licence (Milward 1977: 90). From June 1940 there was tight central control of imports, and by the time an Import Executive was established in December almost all goods from abroad were either bought on government account or shipped in under licence. Overall the volume of imports was reduced by nearly 40 per cent during the war (Aldcroft 1986: 169–70). This helped to simplify the balance of payments problem at a time when there was an increase in world commodity prices and a rise in the demand for imports. It also allowed the government to limit the use of shipping space at a time when a high rate of tonnage was sunk and the costs of shipping and insurance rose sharply. On the negative side, though, it exacerbated shortages of food and other consumer essentials and led to further restrictions on civilian consumption.

The main restriction on consumption was rationing, the scope of which was extended throughout the war after it was introduced in January 1940. It was an effective way of distributing scarce resources fairly, avoiding the unrest which would have come from a widespread perception that producers or suppliers were profiteering. There were some complaints that food rationing failed to take sufficient account of the higher calorific requirements of heavy manual workers, but surveys showed consistently high public approval of the system (Addison 1975: 161–2; Pope 1991: 46–7). Almost all foodstuffs, with the exception of bread and potatoes, were rationed during the war. Some were allocated on a fixed weekly quantity, others were graded on a points system which enabled consumers to choose how to use their allowance and enabled government to adjust the points weighting of items to take account of seasonal factors and shipping losses. In time, household consumer goods and clothing were also rationed under the points system. Alcohol and cigarettes were not rationed, instead they were taxed heavily so that the Exchequer could take advantage of increased spending on these items. The restriction of civilian consumption by rationing helped to reduce inflationary pressures, particularly after the government decided in April 1941 to use subsidies to keep down prices and hopefully prevent workers pressing for large pay increases. By 1945 some £250 million had been spent on food subsidies, much of it financed by the duties on drink and tobacco. The result was that despite severe shortages, food prices rose by only 42 per cent between 1938 and 1946, compared with an increase in personal disposable income of 68 per cent – after direct taxation – over the same period (Milward 1977: 286). Price control was used in other areas to guard against an inflationary wage–price spiral. Rents were frozen on unfurnished property and prices were regulated on the 'utility goods' which first appeared in 1942 – these were household items of government-approved quality and design which were mass-produced at prices which most consumers could afford. Overall, government measures kept the rise in the cost of living below 50 per cent between 1938 and 1945 (Aldcroft 1986: 181).

The extent to which a pre-war civilian market economy was transformed into a wartime state-directed model can be illustrated simply: from 1940 government expenditure on both civil and war needs accounted for at least half the national product (Booth 1989: 45). Financing this level of state expenditure was a serious challenge, particularly for an economy which had recovered only recently from the effects of the world-wide depression. Policy makers were at least fortunate that they could be guided by the lessons of the first world war. Whereas the earlier conflict was financed mainly by borrowing, over half the domestic costs of the war effort from 1939 were met by taxation. This sought to relieve future generations of the burden of crippling war debts and it helped to guard against inflation by acting as a restraint on civilian consumption. In addition to the high duties which consumers paid on items such as alcohol, tobacco and entertainments, there were sizeable increases in direct taxation. The standard rate of income tax was raised from 7s 6d at the start of the war to 10s (50 per cent) in 1941. Higher earners were subject to an increased rate of surtax. Personal allowances and earned income relief were lowered and some 4 million new taxpayers were brought into the system. Partly for financial reasons, but also to prevent the perception that they were profiteering from the war, firms were taxed heavily: an excess profits tax set at 60 per cent in 1939 was raised to 100 per cent in 1940 (Aldcroft 1986: 183).

Even with higher taxation, the government had heavy borrowing requirements; in order to minimise the repayment costs of this borrowing the bank rate was maintained at 2 per cent for most of the war. To ease the burden further, Keynes, a special adviser at the Treasury from July 1940, argued that the government should mobilise the nation's savings, a case he set out in *How to Pay for the War* in 1940. He recognised that marshalling savings either voluntarily or compulsorily would provide a cheap source of funds for the government and help to check inflation by reducing consumer spending. In preparation for the budget of 1941 Keynes, James Meade and Richard Stone compiled the first official survey of national income and expenditure. This allowed the Treasury to calculate how much demand had to be removed from the economy in the form of savings and taxation in order to prevent inflation. As a result, the 1941 budget was designed to promote saving as well as increase taxation. A degree of compulsory saving was introduced, while for the voluntary investor a number of savings instruments were available. These ranged from National Savings for the small investor with funds to place in the Post Office, to Treasury bills for individuals or organisations with larger sums to invest.

Although the majority of funds borrowed in wartime came from internal sources, Britain also built up large external debts by 1945. After a brief attempt to boost exports in the winter of 1939–40 to cover the increased imports bill, the government conceded that normal trading arrangements would not come close to meeting the costs of war. Prudent housekeeping was set aside for the more immediate demands of the contest. Large sterling balances totalling almost £3,500 million were accumulated by the middle of 1945 as Britain piled up debts with colonies, Dominions, countries in the middle east and south America and western European governments in exile (Aldcroft 1986: 187). A massive volume of supply was obtained by this means, but it also turned Britain into a debtor nation on a huge scale which was a burden after the war.

In order to raise dollars for imports from north America overseas assets worth some £1,100 million were sold by Britain, picked off by

American buyers often at below market value. The principal means by which the dollar shortage was overcome, though, was the Lend Lease Agreement of 1941. This arrangement meant that Britain would continue to receive US supplies for as long as they were required even though it could not pay the bills at the time. Supplies obtained under Lend Lease were at a lower level than imports paid for in cash until the end of 1942 (Milward 1984: 68). But at its peak in 1943–4 Lend Lease was supplying about one quarter of the armaments received by British and Empire forces (Aldcroft 1986: 187). It was also a vital source of food and raw materials and freed Britain to concentrate on war production without the need to worry about its export performance during hostilities. In all, some $27 billion worth of purchases were received under the scheme. After allowing for reciprocal aid from Britain of almost $6 billion, Lend Lease still covered over 50 per cent of Britain's total wartime payments deficit (Reynolds 1991: 152). Under the terms of the loan agreed with the US at the end of 1945, the debt for wartime Lend Lease goods was wiped out; payment was only required for those goods left in the pipeline when Lend Lease was cancelled after the defeat of Japan (Milward 1984: 70).

The performance of the war economy

Assessing Britain's wartime economic performance raises immediate conceptual difficulties. Much depends on what is being assessed and the criteria that are to be employed. Judgements could be made solely on the basis of what was required to meet the short-term demands of war, or a longer-term view could be taken of the way in which policy decisions stored up problems for the post-war economy – for example, the neglect of export markets, the sale of dollar-earning assets and the accumulation of sterling balances. The focus could be on the intensity of resource use or it could be on the efficiency of economic mobilisation. A further complication is that the British war economy was not mobilised in isolation: international loans and aid were received from a number of sources, and territories in the Empire and Commonwealth provided labour and materials on favourable terms. A balanced assessment also has to recognise both the context in which resources were mobilised and the constraints which operated on policy. It is likely, for example, that military defeats in 1941–2 exaggerated the perception that there was a crisis in Britain's war production. Also, several key industries had a history of strained industrial relations which could not be forgotten in wartime; many smaller firms had suffered from poor management for years; and the country relied heavily on imports, most of which had to be hauled over very long distances.

It is possible none the less to offer some general conclusions about Britain's wartime economic performance. In comparative terms the degree of labour mobilisation was creditable. By June 1944, 55 per cent of the labour force was either in uniform or in civilian war work, a higher proportion than that achieved in Germany or the United States, but lower than that achieved by the Soviet Union. The percentage of net national income – taking into account external sources as well as domestic finance – mobilised for Britain's war effort climbed sharply, from 16 per cent in 1939 to a peak of 57 per cent in 1943. This compared favourably with the United States, but failed to match Germany and the Soviets, both of whom allocated 76 per cent of their national income to the war effort in 1943 (Harrison 1988: 183–5). Of course Britain relied heavily on external supplies, especially from the United States, but the Soviets were about equally reliant. It should also be remembered at this point that Britain's war effort was disrupted by air-raids and blockade, the Soviets suffered extensive loss of territory and population, but the US were able to organise war production free from such external threats (Harrison 1988: 189, 191). The US also had the advantage of being able to utilise a massive, well-organised and highly productive industrial base – way in advance of the platform on which Britain built its war effort.

The transformation of the British economy for war had to be achieved quickly, because it was only after 1938 that defence requirements took priority over the maintenance of domestic economic stability. Yet by the start of the war Britain had almost matched Germany's defence spending in relative terms, while its production of tanks and aircraft already exceeded German output (Aldcroft 1986: 165). Production levels were heavily affected by strategic priorities and this can make international comparisons difficult. It was no surprise, for example, that British output of medium and heavy bombers was far higher than that of Germany and Japan, both of whom virtually ceased building these aircraft in 1944. But this should not disguise the fact that spectacular increases in output were achieved in wartime Britain in a number of areas: including small arms, shells, high explosives, and wheeled vehicles (Milward 1977: 91). The agricultural sector also performed remarkably well, with more land under cultivation, more labour employed and the balance of crops altered to produce a greater calorific yield per acre of land. Overall, total output in the economy climbed steadily to its peak in 1943, at which point it was about 27 per cent above its immediate pre-war level (Aldcroft 1986: 170).

This productive effort suggested that labour had been mobilised effectively. It was also testimony to the commitment of millions of workers to the war effort, a feature that was illustrated by engineering workers after the British Expeditionary Force had evacuated from Dunkirk in the summer of 1940 without most of its heavy equipment. As invasion threatened, factories worked day and night to provide the supplies for the defence of Britain, encouraged by propaganda which stressed the vital role played by industry in war. Holidays were cancelled, weekends were ignored and the length of shifts was increased, which meant workers frequently completed twelve-hour days seven times a week. In the first week after Dunkirk production rose by a quarter, but after a month the long hours took their toll and output fell back as workers tired (Calder 1992: 117–18). Nevertheless, across the whole economy from 1938 to 1943 output per worker rose by some 10 per cent (Aldcroft 1986: 174).

This is not to say that the labour force was never criticised. Throughout the war there was constant concern about levels of productivity, not least because once resources had been fully mobilised the only way to increase output was to improve productivity. In 1941 Sir John Wardlaw-Milne, the chairman of the Select Committee on National Expenditure, complained that war production had reached only 75 per cent of its maximum. At the start of 1942 *The Times* reported that arms production was 40 per cent below what was possible (Tiratsoo and Tomlinson 1993: 21–2). Critics pointed to alleged deficiencies in the workforce, a charge that was taken up with some force subsequently by Correlli Barnett. In his attempt to expose the weaknesses in Britain's wartime economy and trace the recent origins of the 'British disease', Barnett compared the productivity of British workers unfavourably with their wartime counterparts in Germany and the United States (Barnett 1987: 87, 146). He acknowledged that several factors were responsible – poor management, an education system which failed to produce well-trained industrial workers, a long-term failure to keep pace with advanced technological change – but he also blamed what he believed were faults in the workforce: slackness, absenteeism, lack of work discipline, a willingness to conduct unofficial strikes and the reluctance of skilled workers to abandon restrictive practices. As he pointed out, regular stoppages affected the aircraft, coal and shipbuilding industries, sometimes caused by trivial issues such as canteen facilities or the refusal of management to allow collections for the Red Army during working hours (Barnett 1987: 67–8, 121, 154–6). A large part of the problem, he argued, was the Essential Work Order of 1941, because it restricted the rights of employers to sack workers in certain key industries and removed an important source of discipline in the workplace (Barnett 1987: 76, 115).

Although the workforce was not without its faults during the war, Barnett's criticisms tend to disregard mitigating factors. It should be acknowledged, for instance, that hours of work in Britain were usually longer than in Germany or the United States, which helps to explain why British workers were more prone to absenteeism. Coal-mining, where output fell every year during the war, showed the problems faced by an industry when it lost manpower to the armed forces and was left with an ageing workforce which had to complete large numbers of shifts. In any case, productivity is governed less by the work-rate of the labour force than by the use and quality of capital equipment, an area where Britain was at a disadvantage compared with America and Germany (Parker 1990: 143). It is true that days lost through strikes in Britain were higher every year from 1941 to 1945 than in the last full year of peace, but most of the stoppages were brief and about three-quarters of them were confined to four trades: metals, engineering, coal and shipbuilding. In other industries the strike rate was much lower. It was no coincidence that the strike rate was highest in those industries which had suffered most heavily in the inter-war depression, leaving a legacy of bitterness which continued to affect labour relations during the war. Workers in these industries understandably exploited their enhanced bargaining power during the war to press for improved wages and conditions, especially as it was widely expected that the return of peace would be accompanied by the return of mass unemployment.

By focusing on industrial problems during the war, it is easy to overlook the constructive role which the workforce played in the improvement of productivity. Workers regularly channelled ideas to management about how to increase efficiency through Joint Production Committees (Bullock 1967: 94–5). These were set up voluntarily, with the full support of government, across industry to allow management and workers' representatives to discuss areas of common concern each month. Most were established from 1942, many in the engineering industry; overall some 6,000 Joint Production Committees were set up in wartime and comments on their performance on the whole were positive (Jefferys 1991: 62; Tiratsoo and Tomlinson 1993: 29). Co-operation between all sides in industry seemed to bring some benefits and it appeared to offer lessons for the post-war economy.

The economic legacy of the war

Britain's financial position at the end of the war illustrated starkly that the resources required for victory had been way beyond what the country could afford. When peace returned Britain had the largest external debt in history – the net change on capital account between the outbreak of war and the end of 1945 was £4,700 million (Cairncross 1987: 7). As production had been geared to the war effort, exports had fallen to 40 per cent of their volume in 1938. This moved the balance of payments far into deficit and ensured that Britain would continue to borrow during peacetime. It was calculated that Britain needed to increase its export volume by between 50 and 75 per cent over its pre-war level within five years simply to regain equilibrium (Cairncross 1987: 7). This would be a difficult task, not least because the United States had penetrated former British export markets in Asia and Australasia, and because of the disruption which war had caused to the world economy. The external position was weakened further by the wartime sale of more than £1,000 million worth of dollar-earning assets, which reduced Britain's capacity for invisible earnings and damaged its status as an international banker. To make matters worse, Britain had to continue to finance overseas military expenditure of some £800 million per year, a commitment which could not be reduced quickly because of strategic and political considerations. When Lend Lease was abruptly cancelled after the defeat of Japan, Britain faced what Keynes referred to as a 'financial Dunkirk'; the immediate solution at the end of 1945 was to negotiate a massive loan worth $5,000 million from the United States and Canada.

Financial losses were accompanied by physical damage. Almost 400,000 Britons were killed during the war; if the seriously injured are included the loss to the labour force totalled 750,000. Half a million houses were destroyed or made uninhabitable by air-raids and another 4 million were badly damaged, which amounted to about a third of the pre-war stock. Extensive damage had also been caused to factories, schools, hospitals and other buildings. Enemy attacks meant that Britain's shipping fleet was 28 per cent smaller at the end of the war than it had been before the war, despite a replacement building programme. Finally, there was a deterioration in capital stock caused by the postponement of the renewal of plant and machinery during the war and the neglect of routine maintenance.

The effect of the war on the future of British production was mixed. The scaling down of industrial investment was a problem, particularly in staple industries such as coal and textiles which also faced manpower shortages. The diversion of manpower into the armed forces meant that large numbers of younger workers would have to make up the years of industrial training they had missed while in uniform (Aldcroft 1986: 189). The transfer of resources to war production also meant that civilian industries required substantial expansion as the armed forces were demobilised and peacetime economic conditions returned. On the positive side, though, the war helped to promote both technological change and new managerial techniques in industry (Milward 1984: 18). The pressure of war had led to scientific breakthroughs in areas such as computing, radar, synthetic materials, pharmaceuticals, nuclear fission and jet engines, all of which could be applied to potential growth industries (Aldcroft 1986: 190). Britain also benefited from the way in which agriculture rose to the challenge of war with a major improvement in productivity.

Preparation for the return of a peacetime economy was under way by 1945. As hostilities ended a large number of war contracts had already been terminated, stocks were sold off and factory space decommissioned. Reports produced by the wartime government outlined the main tasks of economic reconstruction and warned of the dangers that lay ahead. Much work remained, however, and the main responsibility for managing the transition to a civilian economy fell to Attlee's Labour government. For pragmatic as much as ideological reasons the new socialist administration favoured only a gradual relaxation of wartime economic controls. State controls over the labour force were largely relinquished, but the maintenance of restrictive controls over investment, imports and prices, together with positive controls over production, was seen as particularly important (Rollings 1992: 28). These were tools which helped the government to confront the economic problems referred to so far, but equally significant was the role they played in the fight against post-war inflation, a serious threat because of the way in which wartime measures had suppressed a vast amount of demand which would became effective as soon as supplies became available in peacetime. It was to combat inflation, as well as ensure social justice, that rationing and price subsidies were continued well into the post-war period.

The way in which Attlee's administration managed the transition to a peacetime economy has been a source of controversy. Much of this was generated by Correlli Barnett, who criticised Labour for failing to remedy the shortcomings in Britain's industrial performance which the war had highlighted. He claimed that Labour, both as members of the coalition and later as a governing party, failed to prioritise economic regeneration and modernisation. Instead they sought to create a 'New Jerusalem', passing a series of social reforms which had been designed in wartime by an 'enlightened Establishment' of academics, churchmen, politicians and journalists, whose left-wing agenda had been popularised by the collective dynamic of war (Barnett 1987: 11–37). In terms of post-war planning, he argued, the balance of Whitehall's collective attention was tipped towards desirable social goals rather than improved industrial performance (Barnett 1987: 263). The result was an expensive welfare apparatus which shielded the British from economic reality, leading to years of low productivity, high overhead costs and relative economic decline – right-wing commentators who shared Barnett's thesis argued that this malaise persisted until the advent of Thatcherism in the 1980s.

However, few interpretations of any aspect of Britain's wartime history have attracted as much negative comment as Barnett's thesis. In the first place, it simply understates Labour's attempts to modernise Britain's industrial base. For example, ministers such as Cripps and Dalton had developed both an understanding of the country's industrial shortcomings and ideas about how they should be tackled during their time in the coalition. As members of Attlee's cabinet these two played a central role in setting up agencies which aimed to promote best practice and improve output and efficiency. Cripps at the Board of Trade established the Production Efficiency Service, which provided a consultancy service on productivity and up-to-date methods. He also continued wartime work on standardisation by creating the Special Research Unit. Together with Dalton he managed at last to secure public money to finance a new British Institute of Management, which aimed to address some of the serious weaknesses in management which had been exposed during the war. An expanded Department of Scientific and Industrial Research and a newly created National Research and Development Council were also important conduits for a post-war government which increased state expenditure on civil research and development five-fold (Tomlinson 1993: 2–4).

Secondly, Barnett's argument underestimates the constraints which operated on the post-war government. The freedom to concentrate on a long-term strategy for economic modernisation was curtailed by the need for an immediate increase in output, particularly in those industries which were central to the export drive, and the fight against a balance of payments deficit. In the meantime, those supply-side measures which the government favoured met constant opposition from a private sector which was largely hostile to Labour. The main concern of private industry in this period was to resist any measures which seemed to resemble creeping nationalisation or which challenged industrial self-government (Mercer 1991: 72). The obvious example of this was the hostility of the Federation of British Industry (FBI) to Development Councils, bodies which drew on the inter-war rationalisation movement and wartime industrial board proposals, but which included equal representation of employers and employees (Morgan 1984: 129; Mercer 1991: 72–3; Tomlinson 1993: 4). Unfortunately, while private industry knew what it was against, it had few constructive suggestions to make about economic reconstruction and modernisation.

The extent to which the organisation of the economy for war helped to produce a 'Keynesian revolution' in policy-making is similarly contentious. According to Sayers, the first Keynesian budget came in 1941: this budget was less a statement of public finance and more an instrument for regulating domestic expenditure and controlling inflation. The theory was that by forecasting the behaviour of the major economic aggregates in the year ahead, it was possible for the Treasury to calculate how much taxation was required to siphon off excess demand in the economy and close the inflationary 'gap' (Sayers 1983: 107–17). Forecasting was not an exact science, but by collecting data on national income and expenditure the Treasury was able to arrive at a decisive 'hunch' about the appropriate level of taxation. This new method of formulating the budget – based on a survey of national income and expenditure and informed by a general theory of the behaviour of economic aggregates – was seen to have important implications for the future. The acceptance of Keynesian theory, at least in part during the war, meant a new role for the budget, a new approach to monetary policy and the setting of interest rates, the monitoring of principal economic aggregates and the use of the resulting data in the making of fiscal as well as monetary policy (Booth 1984: 264).

In addition to the 1941 budget, another apparent milestone on the road to Keynesian policies was the 1944 white paper on employment, which accepted the principle that government had a responsibility for maintaining high and stable employment levels after the war: Keynes had only a limited role in the white paper discussions, but he supported the document as an important step forward (Booth 1983: 111–17). According to Booth, ministers and officials were not converted to Keynesian theory immediately. Indeed, he argued that the post-war Labour government waited until 1947 before it turned to Keynesian prescriptions – ironically to counter inflation rather than create jobs –

and even then it was several more years before Treasury administrators became skilled practitioners of macro-economic demand management (Booth 1983: 121–3). The Keynesian revolution, he cautions, was a highly protracted process.

The very existence of a Keynesian revolution in policy-making, however, has been called into question. Tomlinson noted that Keynesian policy proposals in 1941 and 1947 were acceptable primarily because they were aimed at reducing inflation; this in no way implied that the reverse of the policy – using fiscal policy to create jobs – would have found similar acceptance. Also, higher levels of employment in Britain in the 1950s and 1960s were mainly the product of higher investment and increased exports, not public sector deficits to stimulate demand. In any case, he argued, while governments were able to fine-tune demand, their freedom to accumulate a large public sector deficit was constrained by the negative view which the money markets took of such a course. Keynesian theory clearly affected the discourse of economic policy-making, but market conditions and a host of other external factors limited how far it could affect policy-making in practice (Tomlinson 1984: 259–61). Rollings raised similar objections to Booth's analysis, pointing out that most senior Treasury officials in the 1940s did not understand Keynesian economic theory; if they occasionally favoured policies which had a Keynesian stamp it was for administrative reasons, such as the Treasury's desire to retain control of public spending, not because of theoretical considerations (Rollings 1985: 95–100).

In essence there is a good deal of common ground between these different views. It is agreed, for example, that Keynesian theory came to dominate the discourse of economic policy-making after the war: whether or not Treasury officials understood the theory in full matters less than the fact that they took advice from specialists who did. Also, the reasons why officials supported Keynesian prescriptions are less important than the fact that the techniques and supporting data for implementing such policies were available and used. True, the government's ability to regulate the operation of a complex market economy with Keynesian policies was limited. But it was important none the less that Keynesian theory had altered expectations about what governments could and should achieve by economic management, among politicians, civil service and the private sector. As Keynes himself said, the sentence in which the government recognised full employment as one of its primary aims was worth more than the rest of the 1944 white paper in total (Booth 1983: 114).

Conclusion

After a painful and prolonged inter-war depression, Britain mobilised its economy for war remarkably well after 1939. The labour force, productive capacity and administrative services were all used effectively to supply the war effort. Although some industries saw an increase in strikes, government largely retained the consent and support of the civilian population in its management of the war economy. Rationing, price subsidies and steeply progressive taxation all contributed to the belief that economic policy was based on a principle of 'fair shares'. Indeed, the war witnessed a temporary narrowing of income differentials as unskilled wages rose more than skilled wages, and wages in general rose more than salaries (Summerfield 1986). Of course there were problems. Until the war turned in favour of the Allies in 1942 there was almost constant criticism of apparent shortcomings in production – the culprits identified depended largely on the politics of the person making the charge. The war did expose problems with the quality of Britain's capital stock, production techniques, labour relations and quality of management. But in mitigation there has been a tendency for commentators to compare various features of Britain's wartime economic performance with the most impressive counterpart in each particular field, thereby heightening the impression of British inefficiency and weakness.

Britain emerged from the war dependent on the US for economic support. But the rate at which it recovered economically – albeit with the help of US dollars – was creditable. The idea that Britain would have halted its relative economic decline internationally by favouring an all-out drive for modernisation over the creation of a 'social miracle' has been rejected here: in any case, many western nations who overtook Britain economically in the post-war era devoted a higher proportion of their domestic product to social security expenditure than Britain (Hobsbawm 1993: 22). The post-war Labour government attempted to use some of the lessons that had been learned during the war – including the use of Keynesian policies – to improve Britain's economic performance. But the fundamental weaknesses in the British economy long pre-dated the second world war, and correcting these weaknesses has proved beyond the capacity of any post-war government.

Chapter 4

Wartime media – press, radio and cinema

The willingness of civilians to contribute to the war effort was a matter of decisive military importance because Britain's armed forces depended on the industrial and organisational skills of the home population. The responsibility for maintaining civilian morale fell to the Ministry of Information (MOI), which began work in September 1939 but which had been planned since 1935. It attempted to counter the efforts of Goebbels's Ministry of Popular Enlightenment and Propaganda, though the MOI's title deliberately implied that the Ministry was engaged primarily in disseminating information, not in social control or political indoctrination. The first Minister of Information, Lord Macmillan, summarised for the cabinet in 1939 the three central messages which were to be carried to the public: what Britain was fighting for; how Britain was fighting; and the need for sacrifice if the fight was to be won. Macmillan's stewardship of the Ministry was generally regarded as a failure and his two successors – Sir John Reith and Duff Cooper – fared little better. In fact the MOI attracted intense criticism in the first two years of the war; it was seen to be expensive, bureaucratic, overstaffed and ineffective; the patronising tone of its early efforts was captured in a poster which read, '*YOUR* courage, *YOUR* cheerfulness, *YOUR* resolution, will bring us victory' – people were entitled to ask what the Ministry meant by 'you' and 'us'. It was only when Brendan Bracken became Minister of Information in July 1941 that the MOI began to operate effectively, working well with the three main branches of the wartime media to support civilian morale.

The national press

It was in the interest of the wartime government to maintain cordial relations with the press, especially as the demand for war news was to push aggregate newspaper sales above their pre-war level. At the peak of circulation it was estimated that four out of five men and two out of three women read at least one paper each day, despite higher prices, distribution problems caused by a disrupted transport network and a reduction in the size of papers because of the shortage of newsprint (Koss 1984: 602). It was also clear, though, that freedom of the press could not survive the outbreak of war; censorship in some form had to be employed, not least because of the need to safeguard information which might have been of military value to the enemy. Operating a system of censorship without alienating the press was a challenge which frequently defeated ministers and officials. Relations between press and government became strained in the early stages of the conflict, creating a climate of mutual suspicion which took some time to evaporate.

The initial point of controversy was the tight control which the authorities exercised over official information. In September 1939, for example, the MOI withheld news that the British Expeditionary Force had left for the continent, even though this was public knowledge in France and the United States (Stammers 1983: 137). In October the accreditation and monitoring of war correspondents proved so restrictive that about 100 neutral reporters made their way to Berlin, where they found it easier to obtain reliable information about the war than they had in Britain or France (Knightley 1975: 220). At this stage of the war tight control of information was combined with a voluntary system of censorship in which editors sought guidance from the Censorship Division about the handling of potentially sensitive material. Subjects on which advice should be sought before publication were brought to the attention of editors by the issue of Defence ('D') Notices. These prevented newspaper discussion of the movement of troops, armour and munitions, the whereabouts of prisoners of war, current or projected military operations and wider defence measures such as fortifications (McLaine 1979: 25). In certain circumstances these restrictions were obviously justifiable; the problem for the press was the tendency of the service ministries to interpret guidelines on censorship in all circumstances in the most restrictive way possible. As a result columnists were often unable to discuss the progress of the war in a serious way, so they vented their frustration instead on official bureaucracy and the shortcomings of the Ministry of Information – commonly referred to as the Ministry of Aggravation.

Although there was a commitment to a voluntary code, Regulation 39B of the pre-war Emergency Powers (Defence) Act gave the authorities general powers of censorship which could be called upon whenever circumstances warranted. In May 1940 the new coalition government responded to the changed circumstances brought about by Hitler's attack on the west and extended controls over the press. From this point forward censorship was widened to cover critical opinion as well as sensitive information. The most significant measure in this respect was Regulation 2D, which enabled the Home Secretary to act against material which in his view was calculated to foment opposition to the war, without any right of appeal for the offending publication. The first major victim of the coalition's more stringent approach was the communist paper, the *Daily Worker*, the export of which was prohibited in May 1940. By November 1940 an export ban had been applied to nine newspapers or periodicals, most of which had communist or left-wing sympathies (Stammers 1983: 134). Attlee told the Commons that criticisms of the government or military leadership endangered the war effort by threatening to undermine public morale. But this argument was contentious for two main reasons. First, ministers may well have been sensitive to criticism, but there was no evidence that adverse comment about the government's performance necessarily damaged morale in the country. Second, restriction of free comment conflicted with the official portrayal of the war as a defence of democracy against totalitarianism.

The latter consideration helps to explain why ministers attempted to regulate press coverage wherever possible by discreet approaches to newspaper proprietors and editors. The use of informal channels enabled the government to influence newspaper comment in private while maintaining in public a commitment to press freedom. In October 1940, for instance, Churchill asked the Liberal minister Sir Archibald Sinclair to use his influence with the *News Chronicle* to stop publication of what he believed were 'mischievous' articles. In the same month Attlee and Beaverbrook threatened representatives of the Newspaper Proprietors Association with compulsory censorship if the *Daily Mirror* and *Sunday Pictorial* continued to criticise the government (Stammers 1983: 141–2). Both of these Mirror group papers had a reputation for challenging authority, taking a populist stance against what could loosely be described as the 'establishment'. Their criticism of appeasement and the Chamberlain government had helped to bring Churchill to power in 1940 – indeed in the immediate pre-war period Churchill had been invited to write for both papers. It was ironic, therefore, that in 1941 the Prime Minister continued to complain regularly to Cecil King, an executive director of Mirror newspapers, about his papers' coverage of the war effort (Cudlipp 1953: 142–153; King 1970: 94–106).

There were occasions, though, when more direct methods of press censorship were used in place of behind-the-scenes approaches by ministers. Once more the main target was the *Daily Worker*, publication of which was suppressed from January 1941 to August 1942. At the time it was suppressed the *Daily Worker* regarded the war as a capitalist venture against the interests of the working class. It also claimed that Britain might find it impossible to win the war. But the main charge against the paper was that it undermined public morale and thus the war effort by its criticisms of the government and ministers, several of whom were subject to personal attacks in its columns. The paper's principal target was the shortcomings of policy on the home front. The *Daily Worker* campaigned for more deep-shelter provision, better ARP services, better rates of compensation, the commandeering of large houses and the opening up of large private shelters (McLaine 1979: 190). Home Intelligence, however, found no evidence that the editorial policy of the *Daily Worker* undermined public morale. The paper in fact accounted for less than 1 per cent of total national daily circulation and had little influence beyond the limited sphere of its communist readership (Curran and Seaton 1997: 61). Suppression served mainly to exaggerate the significance of the paper and allowed British communists to present themselves as martyrs, victimised because they spoke out against a powerful wartime government. In all probability, the only morale that was damaged by the *Daily Worker* was that of ministers who were sensitive to criticism.

The most sensitive of all to criticism was the Prime Minister, who it appears initiated much of the war cabinet discussion on the need to exercise greater control over newspapers. Although Churchill had worked as a journalist and was an avid reader of the press, his attitude towards most reporters and columnists was close to contempt. He did not meet the lobby correspondents, nor did he give background briefings to journalists on or off the record. His sensitivity to negative comment was so acute that he even objected to newspapers reporting speeches by MPs which were critical of the wartime government or the military: the MOI responded by blacking out offending passages (Margach 1978: 66–70). As before, Churchill's main complaints were aimed at the *Daily Mirror*, a paper whose populist instincts were given free expression during wartime: it fully supported the war effort, but it pilloried ministers, commanding officers or industrialists who it believed were letting down the national cause. The *Mirror* had an average circulation of 1.9 million, a readership that was drawn by the paper's combination of lively human interest stories, popular features and hard-hitting columns by 'Cassandra' – William Connor. It was also the paper of the citizen soldier, providing a voice for the massed ranks of conscripts through the frequent use of readers' letters and a regular forces column. The paper's identification with the other ranks lent added weight to its criticisms of 'brasshats, blimps and boneheads' in the officer class, too many of whom it believed had been promoted on the basis of social connections rather than merit.

The *Mirror*'s habit of blaming military blunders and deficiencies in central organisation for the sequence of British defeats in 1941 and early 1942 was a constant irritant for Churchill. In March 1942 matters came to a head when the *Mirror* printed a powerful cartoon by Philip Zec, featuring a shipwrecked merchant sailor clinging to a raft in an empty sea with a caption that read: 'The price of petrol has been increased by one penny – official'. The cartoon was open to several interpretations, but Zec's intention was to highlight the need to conserve petrol by showing the human cost involved in shipping oil to Britain. Churchill and cabinet colleagues, however, believed that the drawing implied that the government was allowing petrol companies to profiteer from the oil shortages caused by shipping losses. At a time when military defeats caused the government to fear for its political survival, the decision was taken to make an example of the *Daily Mirror*. Churchill and several senior members of the war cabinet supported immediate suppression of the paper. But the matter was referred to a Special Committee, chaired by Sir John Anderson, which decided against suppression. It was agreed instead that the Home Secretary would issue a public warning in parliament, threatening the *Mirror* with closure if it continued to print what the government regarded as 'unwarranted and malignant' criticism. Morrison told the House that pro-war papers which criticised the government could be closed down under Regulation 2D, even if there was no suspicion that their intention was to undermine the war effort. The warning to the *Mirror* reminded other proprietors that the government was prepared to use sanctions against national newspapers, not simply against smaller publications such as the *Daily Worker* (Curran and Seaton 1997: 64–5).

In retrospect the government's heavy-handed tactics were probably unjustified. There was little persuasive evidence from Home Intelligence that critical comment in the *Daily Mirror* damaged morale, weakened army discipline or undermined industrial relations. The government's action was condemned by members of both houses of parliament, several of whom argued that state interference with the press should be kept to a minimum in order to safeguard morale: press freedom was an essential feature of democracy and its maintenance in wartime was a symbol of the legitimacy of the war effort. Most other newspapers rallied to the defence of the *Mirror*, pointing out that freedom to criticise the government was more likely to help rather than hinder the search for victory. The episode confirmed how sensitive ministers had become to criticism and arguably reminded observers that there was good reason to ask serious questions about the performance of the government by early 1942.

Assessing the effect of the warning on Fleet Street is difficult. No sanctions were applied to the *Mirror* or any other major title after March 1942, possibly reflecting a more circumspect approach by editors after Morrison's warning (Stammers 1983: 152). Alternatively, the voices raised in defence of the *Mirror* could have persuaded ministers that direct attacks on press freedom would be counter-productive. Equally, a return to more discreet methods of influencing the press could have been caused by a growing sense of self-confidence within government after the success of the allied operations in north Africa in late 1942. In any case, the authorities did not need to control newspapers directly. All the major titles supported the war effort and shared the same cause as the government. The MOI still maintained a tight control over the release of war news, helped by journalists who were prepared to follow the official line uncritically, functioning as cheerleaders and propagandists rather than independent reporters (Knightley 1975: 304–33). And most important of all, the government already controlled the main channel of communication in the country, the BBC.

The BBC

There was never any doubt that the functions of the Ministry of Information and the BBC would interlock in wartime. In 1939 the Home Secretary had told the Commons that in the event of war the government would leave the BBC to carry on, but with a very close liaison between themselves and the Ministry of Information and definite regulations about how broadcasting should operate (Briggs 1995: 83–4). The BBC was determined to preserve some autonomy, but this was conditional upon the maintenance of good relations with government. In practice there was only nominal retention of the Corporation's independence, with ministers having final authority over broadcasting policy. The government could veto the appearance of any broadcaster whose views it found objectionable, it also controlled the content of political statements and news coverage on the BBC. Ultimately, the Corporation was the government's official channel of communication, carrying out instructions from the MOI and aware of the role it had to play in the mobilisation of the civilian war effort and the maintenance of morale.

The output of the BBC during the war was confined to the radio as television broadcasting was suspended throughout the conflict – in 1939 there were some 9 million licensed wireless sets in the country. According to the most recent account of the wartime BBC, radio broadcasts contributed to the war effort in three main ways. First, they disseminated information in a straightforward manner to a mass audience. This information could range from ministerial announcements, to news from the battlefield, to advice on issues such as food preparation, health, national savings or conserving fuel. Next, they reflected the concerns, hopes and fears of ordinary people, whose voices were regularly carried across the airwaves in programmes broadcast from factories, civil defence units and army barracks. Finally, they helped to shape public attitudes and lead public debate about post-war issues (Nicholas 1996). In this sense the BBC became an important instrument of war, constantly emphasising that everyone had his or her own contribution to make to the national effort. It also functioned as a common reference point for civilians and soldiers, bringing people together as they listened to the same news items, programmes or the inspirational broadcasts of Churchill.

At the start of the war there was only one programme for home listeners. The emphasis was on meeting the expected demand for news, particularly as it was predicted that German air-raids would begin immediately. When these predictions were confounded and the 'bore war' developed, broadcasters found that there was little news to report. The result was widespread criticism of the Corporation's lacklustre effort in the early weeks. With the BBC failing to satisfy its audience the way was open for Lord Haw Haw to become the first radio star of the war, broadcasting German propaganda from Hamburg. At his peak he attracted some 30 per cent of the listening public, most of whom claimed that they tuned in for entertainment rather than because they believed he was telling the truth (Curran and Seaton 1997: 132). Nevertheless, the BBC was sufficiently concerned about Lord Haw Haw to schedule some of their most popular programmes after the main evening news in an effort to prevent listeners tuning in to Hamburg (Briggs 1995: 135). Haw Haw's audience declined in the aftermath of Dunkirk, a period when there was a real hunger for news and the reputation of BBC wartime reporting was established. Most of the public from this point forward used the radio rather than the press as their main source of news, and by February 1941 Listener Research found that nearly two-thirds of civilians considered BBC news to be 100 per cent reliable (Nicholas 1996: 205).

There were occasional complaints. The destruction caused during the blitz was frequently downplayed; hostile comments came from the provinces about 'Londoncentric' reporting; bad news was often released slowly over a period of time; and the MOI continued throughout the war to embargo news from evening broadcasts in deference to the morning papers – the result was that news as important as a cabinet reshuffle could be announced on foreign stations before it was heard on the BBC. More seriously, the disastrous raid on Dieppe in 1942 was reported in a highly selective and unduly positive way and the following year the BBC failed to report all that it knew about the Nazi policy of exterminating Jews. For the most part, though, the Corporation refused to act as a propaganda arm of government: it would report selectively but it would not broadcast deliberate falsehoods. Of course it was reliant on information from various government departments, some of which proved less than accurate. For example, in the Battle of Britain the BBC joined its German equivalent, Deutschlandsender, in reporting distorted figures for aircraft losses: the British overstated their position by 55 per cent, the Germans by 234 per cent (Briggs 1995: 261–2). But despite such lapses the BBC earned the trust of its audience. Moreover, it responded to the demands of war with technical innovations which increased the quality of its reporting; the most notable feature was the improvement of outside broadcast facilities, bringing alive the allied advance after D-Day for a civilian population which could now listen to correspondents' dispatches sent from the front line.

Because of the propaganda value at stake, the BBC's treatment of Allies and enemies alike was supervised by the MOI. During the 'phoney war' the BBC followed the Ministry's practice of discriminating between the German people and the Nazi party, still clinging on to the hope that Hitler's regime would be overthrown from within. After the invasion of the west, though, this distinction was abandoned; it was to be resumed only if a revolutionary situation developed in Germany. In the meantime the watchful eye of the BBC was extended to composers from Germany, Italy and other enemy countries, whose music was banned from the radio. This applied mainly to work which was in copyright because the prime concern of the BBC was to avoid paying royalties to enemy nationals, not to protect listeners from unsafe foreign influences (Nicholas 1996: 156). After the USSR became an ally of Britain in 1941 the BBC responded with enthusiasm, packing the *Radio Times* with tributes to Russian workers. But under pressure from Churchill it played down talk of a second front to help the Soviets. It also decided against broadcasting the *Internationale* in its Sunday evening concert of national anthems, eventually dropping the programme to prevent further embarrassment (Curran and Seaton 1997: 147). Later broadcasts which dealt with the USSR focused on the heroic efforts of the Russian people and carefully avoided paying any credit to the communist system which had contained and eventually turned back Hitler's troops in Europe. The government's sensitivity over the portrayal of the Soviet system was heightened as the debate about post-war reconstruction gathered momentum, shaped in part by the BBC.

The first significant contribution to this debate came on the Sunday after Dunkirk, when J. B. Priestley began his series of *Postscript* broadcasts. In a rich Yorkshire accent, very different from the normal middle-class speaking voice of the BBC, Priestley offered reassurance to listeners, using rural images and references to popular history to persuade them that they could cope with the crisis to come. As well as invoking the nation's past, though, he also summoned its future, encouraging listeners to think about the aims of Britain's war effort. These talks were tinged with sentimentality and focused on generalities rather than a specific policy agenda, but Priestley's appeals for social justice and the communal use of resources had a powerful impact. Certainly his views disturbed some Conservatives who argued that both Priestley and the BBC were becoming unacceptably politicised. Although both the BBC and the MOI denied that he was censored, Priestley's *Postscript* broadcasts were eventually taken off the air.

Discussion of reconstruction and planning for the peace nevertheless continued on the airwaves. In September 1940 *Taking Stock* began as a series of twelve discussion programmes on the state of the nation; in the first months of 1941 there were a number of programmes on planning and rebuilding Britain's urban centres after the damage of the blitz; and in October 1941 *Making Plans* discussed how reconstruction would affect ordinary citizens (Nicholas 1996: 245–8). After helping to launch the Beveridge Report, the BBC carried forward discussion of post-war plans in *The World We Want* in October 1943, *Homes for All* in spring 1944 and *Jobs for All* the following December, all of which were positive about the state's ability to deliver social and economic transformation after the war.

Visions of post-war reform could provide inspiration and encourage national morale. But serious output and home front propaganda had to be leavened with a liberal dose of light entertainment, particularly in a long war which was characterised by hardship, monotony and privation. After the worthy but dull programming of the early weeks of the war the BBC's provision of entertainment found its range. The critical development here came in January 1940 with the start of the Forces Programme, the output of which was designed specifically for the citizen soldiers listening in their units and looking for some light diversion from the routines of service life. It showed that the BBC had developed a greater sensitivity to the requirements of its varied audiences and could provide what people wanted, not necessarily what the Corporation thought they needed. It was in this spirit that the BBC's most popular wartime programmes were developed: *It's That Man Again*, which gently parodied the war effort; *Ack Ack – Beer Beer*, which harnessed the talents of civil defence workers on Anti-Aircraft and Balloon Command sites; *Music While You Work*, playing up-tempo music to industrial workers; *Sincerely Yours*, in which Vera Lynn provided a sentimental link between servicemen overseas and their lovers at home; *Brains Trust*, a chance for a panel of experts to answer a range of questions from the public, mainly of a scientific or philosophical nature with the occasional light-hearted tester for a change of tone; *Band Waggon* and *Hi Gang* and a host of variety shows which could draw audiences of more than 10 million. These and other popular shows on both the Forces Programme and the Home Service helped to maintain spirits and contributed to the 'good war' which the BBC experienced – assisted of course by the fact that the Corporation had only one main rival in the media as a provider of entertainment.

Cinema

Film was one of the most powerful mediums of communication and therefore propaganda during the war. In an age before mass ownership of television, cinema-going was a main leisure activity and an ideal way for people to escape from the reality of life on the wartime home front; it was particularly popular among the working class and adolescents. Although cinemas were closed at the start of the conflict as a defence against air-raids, they were re-opened within a few days by a government which recognised the role that films could play in the maintenance of morale. Weekly cinema attendances during the war reached 25 to 30 million, despite a large increase in seat prices caused in part by the wartime entertainments tax. Most of the films shown in Britain at this time were imports from America, but British film-makers responded to the challenge of war with such success that the 1940s is frequently referred to as a golden age of British cinema.

The production of wartime propaganda films was overseen by the Films Division of the MOI, the main function of which was to liaise with commercial studios, independent producers and newsreel companies. The Films Division commissioned work, advised on the suitability of projects and helped with the logistics of film-making, such as obtaining film stock or securing the release of artists from the armed services. Jack Beddington, who took over as Director of the Films Division in April 1940, made sure that responsibility for propaganda films remained with his organisation rather than with the film industry itself, but he did this without sacrificing too much goodwill from the studios. After taking over the GPO Film Unit – later renamed the Crown Film Unit – from the Post Office in the same month that Beddington took charge, the Films Division began to produce its own films. Most of these were documentaries, made by a roster of producers and directors which included Alberto Cavalcanti, Humphrey Jennings, Harry Watt, Jack Holmes, Stuart Legg, Pat Jackson and Jack Lee. The primary role of the Films Division, though, was to apply the general principles of British propaganda to the cinema, deciding which messages and themes should be emphasised at different stages of the war.

A range of forms and genres was used to convey propaganda to cinema audiences. According to the MOI the newsreels were the most effective form of film propaganda, so these were given priority in the allocation of film stock. The Press and Censorship Division controlled the flow of information to the newsreel companies, but these were left alone in the main to interpret the material which they had been permitted to use (Chapman 1998: 251–2). One noticeable development here was that the tone of newsreel commentaries became more aggressive than any other form of film propaganda (Coultass 1984: 9). Closely related to newsreels was the social realism of the documentary, a genre which developed between the wars and which flourished after 1939. Documentaries were particularly effective at showing audiences how the war was being fought. Films such as *Britain at Bay*, *Britain Can Take It!* and *Christmas Under Fire* carried the message that the country was coping with the crisis of 1940; *Target for Tonight*, an account of a bombing raid on Germany, reassured audiences that Britain was hitting back in 1941; and as the tide of the war turned in favour of the Allies in

1942 the Army Film and Photographic Unit celebrated military success in feature-length documentaries such as *Desert Victory* and *Tunisian Victory*.

Documentaries which simply imparted information – albeit from a particular perspective – were most popular with audiences. Less favoured were the MOI's own short films which exhorted the public to even greater wartime effort or which carried specific messages or instructions from the government. Some 1,400 of these were produced or sponsored by the MOI, given free to exhibitors to include in their programmes and carried round the country in cinema vans for special screenings to ensure that they reached the widest possible audience. Unfortunately for the MOI research showed that most of the public soon became cynical about overt propaganda and resented having to sit through official lectures. The type of propaganda material which worked for audiences in the crisis months of 1940 was not so well suited to later phases of the war. It was in recognition of this that the Films Division altered its policy in 1942, replacing the weekly five-minute film with a monthly fifteen-minute film, designed in the main to meet the public's demand for information and understanding about the progress of the conflict (Chapman 1998: 108–11). As with the shorter pieces, audience reaction to the fifteen-minute versions varied from film to film. According to the most recent survey the overall success rate of MOI film propaganda was uneven: the short films were not as unpopular as commentators often suggest, but too often the audience failed to recognise the message that the films were attempting to convey (Chapman 1998: 106, 113).

Audiences were often resistant to overt propaganda because what they wanted from the cinema was entertainment. Commentators usually therefore regard feature films as the most effective medium of cinema propaganda because the best could integrate messages and themes into an interesting story. At the start of the war the main inspiration for propaganda features came from the studios rather than the MOI. The early pictures emphasised the moral superiority of Britain's cause and downplayed the scale of the effort which would be required to defeat the enemy. Alexander Korda's *The Lion has Wings* used documentary and newsreel footage and featured a reconstruction of the bombing raid on the Kiel Canal, overlaid with patriotic exhortation from Queen Elizabeth – played by Flora Robson – and a voicing of 'decent' British attitudes to the war by Merle Oberon (Coultass 1984: 11; Murphy 1992: 8). Although it was a rather stilted piece, critics on the whole received it favourably and the public made it the most popular film of November 1939. John and Roy Boulting's *Pastor Hall*, released in 1940, was based on the true story of Martin Niemoller, a German priest whose defiance of the Nazis was punished by detention in a concentration camp. The film contrasted the brutality of German Nazis with the more humane values of ordinary Germans, holding out the hope that internal resistance to Hitler's regime would lead to the downfall of the Nazi state. A similar message was present in *Pimpernel Smith*, one of the most popular war films of 1941, but thereafter the distinction between Germans and Nazis ceased to be a theme of British feature films.

War films were popular in the first few years of the conflict. In large part this reflected the continued novelty of the struggle, but it also owed something to the quality of several of the features produced. Michael Powell's *49th Parallel*, finally released in 1941 after a long period in production, was perhaps the first classic British wartime film, winning an Academy Award for best original screenplay. It also provided the most noteworthy example of direct collaboration between the MOI and the film industry during the war (Chapman 1998: 72). It told the story of the crew of a sunken U-boat as they attempted to cross Canada and make their way to the still neutral United States. The differences between the Nazi ideology they represented and the liberal democratic values of the Canadian and English characters they encountered were thrown into sharp relief as the crew resorted to brutal methods to avoid capture. Ultimately the film shows that the representatives of democratic culture could combine quiet decency with great courage, sufficient at least to defeat the Nazis in their midst. Powell was able to pursue this theme without drawing stereotypes; moreover, the strength of the narrative, the spectacular location shots and a powerful cast dominated by Laurence Olivier and Leslie Howard ensured that the film recovered its production costs within three months. Other films such as Charles Frend's *The Foreman Went to France* and Noel Coward and David Lean's *In Which We Serve*, both released in 1942, also managed to achieve both critical acclaim and strong audience appeal. Shortly after victory in Europe had been secured the most popular war film of all made during wartime was released: Anthony Asquith and Terence Rattigan's *The Way to the Stars*.

Mass-Observation's research, though, showed that the kind of entertainment most audiences favoured was escapist. Gainsborough Pictures appreciated this better than any other studio, producing comedies and melodramas which were often scorned by critics but which generated enormous profits. Given the popularity of radio comedy and its stars, humorous films starring the likes of Arthur Askey and Tommy Trinder could be expected to find a large audience. Less predictable was the success of the Gainsborough melodramas such as *The Man in Grey* (1943), *Fanny by Gaslight* (1944), *Love Story* (1944) and *The Wicked Lady* (1945). As recent commentators have observed, though, these pictures have an appeal because they represent a tradition of garish and flamboyant cinema, focusing on the bizarre and the exotic in vaguely historical settings. Women were also drawn to the films because their plots revolved around strong female characters, many of whom were hedonistic and boldly sexual (Murphy 1992: 56; McKibbin 1998: 448). Despite the best efforts of British film-makers, however, the most popular film of the war years was Hollywood's *Gone with the Wind*, on general release from 1942 and shown in London's West End until spring 1944. No British production could match the scale, sweep or glamour of this film which met so completely the need of audiences to lose themselves for a few hours and forget about the war. The only consolation for the English, perhaps, was that three of the four principal stars of *Gone with the Wind* – Vivien Leigh, Olivia De Havilland and Leslie Howard – were English-born.

Conclusion

Despite some initial difficulties Britain's propaganda campaign can be judged an overall success. Press, radio and cinema played their part in victory, assisted for the most part by a Ministry of Information whose performance improved the longer the war continued. There were of course strained relations and complaints from all sides at various times, but in the circumstances co-operation between government and the media functioned fairly smoothly throughout six years of war. The audience, too, played its part. Government messages were not simply carried via the media to a passive public; rather the audience helped to shape the message by making their preferences, values and attitudes known – for example, in surveys conducted by the MOI or BBC, by writing letters to the press, or simply by making commercial decisions about which newspapers to buy or which films to watch. The result was a partial democratisation of the wartime media, a process which was significant in the longer term. Admittedly Fleet Street, Wardour Street and the BBC continued to be dominated by a particular social caste of males during and after the war, but there was a sense none the less in which the content and tone of press and broadcasting became slightly less pompous, stuffy and patronising during the war. The *Daily Mirror* found its populist voice in the conflict and provided a model for others to follow; the BBC began to cater for the demands of its audience and scaled down its mission of national self-improvement; and British films lost some of their obsession with middle-class mores and accents, portraying working-class characters in a more natural and less stereotyped way.

All of this of course ran alongside official encouragement of 'high' culture. The Council for the Encouragement of Music and the Arts (CEMA), a body which later became the Arts Council, was set up in 1940. Its aim was the preservation in wartime of the 'highest standards' in music, drama and painting, and the promotion of these arts to a wider audience. In part this reflected the importance of the myth of 'Deep England' during the war: the idea that at its heart England was not an urban, industrial nation, but a green and pleasant land with rolling hills, village greens and parish churches. Implicit here was the message that no amount of German bombs could destroy the nation's idyllic landscape – which symbolised order, stability, and tradition, linking the past with the present (Calder 1991; Hewison 1995). In propaganda terms, this shows how the war was presented as a fight to defend the country's heritage as well as its future. In cultural terms the myth of 'Deep England', together with the presentation of the British in the mass media, help us to understand the importance of the second world war in the construction of national identity. It was, after all, wartime propaganda that helped to cement the self-image of the British as steadfast, resolute, good-humoured and understated; fifty years after the conflict this self-evaluation continues to have some popular resonance.

Chapter 5

Wartime strategy – Britain and its Allies

Military histories of the second world war explore almost every conceivable aspect of the campaign in every conceivable format: from scholarly works to popular narratives, from global surveys to micro studies. In Britain the most influential history was written by Winston Churchill, whose war memoirs at once gained a semi-official status because of the authority of Churchill as a wartime leader, because he published his version of events so soon after the end of the conflict, and because his commentaries made extensive use of government papers. The memoirs helped to shape a number of assumptions about Britain's conduct of the war. They popularised the idea that the fight against Germany was a crusade for democracy against totalitarianism. Underpinning this was the belief that Britain sought to defeat its enemies from the start and never considered the possibility of a negotiated peace, a defiant stance which apparently intensified after May 1940. In pursuit of victory the memoirs describe an almost unbroken sequence of wise strategic decisions. Finally, the most powerful assumption of all was the certainty that the price of Britain's victory in 1945 was worth paying.

These 'common-sense' views retain a popular hold, buttressed by the work of admiring historians who have helped to shape the Churchill myth. Revisionist historians, though, present a different version of the conduct of the war, questioning both the handling of strategy and the wisdom of remaining in the war for the duration. Much of the recent and sometimes controversial historiography on Britain's wartime strategy focuses on those decisions which were made after the formation of the 'Grand Alliance' in 1941, when the Soviet Union and the United States entered the war. British military historians also tend to concentrate on the Allied campaigns in Europe and north Africa. This is not to deny the importance of the war in the Far East, nor to disregard the British and Imperial troops who fought in that theatre. Instead it simply recognises that responsibility for the defeat of Japan lay overwhelmingly with the United States and that Britain had little influence over strategic decision-making in the Far East – and even the US only devoted 15 per cent of its war effort to the conflict with Japan, with the remainder directed at the war with Germany (Overy 1996: 321). This chapter will therefore examine the main debates about Britain's conduct of wartime strategy, with the focus on the campaign in the west.

Britain and France, September 1939–June 1940

Britain's declaration of war on Germany came two days after Hitler's forces had attacked Poland on 1 September 1939. France followed Britain with its own declaration and these were then joined by the Dominions of Australia, New Zealand, Canada and – after a good deal of hesitation – South Africa. The British effectively declared war on behalf of India, an action which caused enormous resentment, but no amount of pressure from the British was ever sufficient to persuade the Irish Free State to enter the conflict. Although Poland was the immediate cause of the declaration it was decided from the start that Polish independence could not be saved. German forces enjoyed overwhelming strategic, numerical and material advantages over the Poles; moreover, the Germans acted in co-operation with the Soviet Union, whose forces invaded Poland on 17 September to claim the territory allocated to them in the Nazi–Soviet pact of August 1939. Faced with two great hostile powers, Polish resistance collapsed by the end of September. Britain and France had sent supplies to the Poles, but not the meaningful military support which was expected. It has been suggested that this was a serious error, because an attack on Germany's western border at the outbreak of war could have been successful. German defences in the west were stretched thinly during the Polish campaign and an Allied victory at this stage might have encouraged German dissident generals to act against Hitler (Lamb 1993: 15–16).

However, neither the British nor the French favoured early aggressive action against Germany. Chamberlain believed that the Germans could be forced to abandon their territorial ambitions in Europe without a major land war in the west. Intelligence reports reinforced his view that rearmament had seriously weakened the German economy, creating shortages of raw materials and foreign exchange which might prove crucial after twelve or eighteen months. Chamberlain hoped to use the navy as the main instrument of victory, enforcing economic blockade, strangling Germany's home front and causing the internal collapse of Hitler's regime. In the meantime there would be continued rearmament and military preparation. This defensive strategy was endorsed by the French, whose army was still viewed by the British as the ultimate barrier to German advance in the west. The French in the early part of the war concentrated on reinforcing the Maginot line, their series of fortifications along the frontier with Germany. For Britain and France, the risk of an early defeat in the field outweighed the potential benefits of an early victory, the priority at this stage was to convince Germany that it could not succeed against the Anglo-French alliance.

In October 1939 the Germans offered to talk peace with Britain and France. Hitler launched a public 'peace offensive' while Hermann Goering, commander of the Luftwaffe, explored the possibility of a compromise settlement in private talks with intermediaries. Some influential figures were receptive to these soundings. The leaders of Canada, South Africa and New Zealand encouraged Britain to explore avenues which might avert full-scale war; Queen Wilhelmina of Holland and King Leopold of Belgium told King George VI they were willing to act as mediators; a group of Labour MPs called on Chamberlain to hold conference talks with Germany; and later Lord Beaverbrook made clear his support for a compromise peace (Lamb 1993: 17–19). In the autumn of 1939, however, political leaders in Britain and France had no intention of signing a deal which did not involve major German concessions: they insisted on the restoration of Czechoslovakia and Poland, the French wanted to include the restoration of an independent Austria, the British meanwhile set as a precondition the elimination of Hitler and his regime. To accept a deal which did not include these concessions would have made a nonsense of the initial decision to go to war, particularly at a time when Anglo-French forces had barely been tested. As for the Germans there was simply no reason for them to surrender any of the gains made so far, especially with the western Allies so reluctant to take offensive action. Neither was there any prospect of Hitler relinquishing power or being forced aside, despite the faith which the British continued to place at this stage in the German opposition. The 'peace offensive' came to nothing.

As the Anglo-French army continued its defensive preparations and Hitler postponed his attack on the west, the sea became the main arena of war. German U-boats attacked Allied shipping with repeated success, obstructing supply routes and preparing the way perhaps for a future invasion of Britain. The Allies, meanwhile, patrolled the sea lanes in an attempt to enforce blockade. It was during this period that each side came to view Scandinavia and its coastline as an area of major strategic significance. Sweden was important as the main provider of iron-ore for Germany's steel industry. In the summer this iron-ore was shipped from the Swedish port of Lulea, but when ice made this route impossible in winter it was taken by rail to Narvik in Norway and shipped to Germany along the Norwegian coastline. Germany saw that control of Scandinavia would safeguard their supply of a vital raw material; also, occupation of Norway and Denmark would provide ports from which the German navy could break out of the confines of the North Sea and into the Atlantic, an important consideration in the war against British sea-power. For Britain and France, Scandinavian waters could be used to block Germany's supply of iron-ore from Sweden, weakening the enemy's economy and undermining its war effort.

In spring 1940 each side went on the offensive in Scandinavia. On 8 April four British destroyers mined Norwegian waters around Narvik. On the same day, German troops landed in Norway and began to take control of ports, airfields and the main centres of population. With Denmark now subjugated as part of the same operation, German forces were well placed to defeat the relatively small Norwegian army and to resist Allied landings around the town of Trondheim. Unable to wrest the initiative from the Germans, who controlled the main airfields, the Allies were forced to evacuate Norway only weeks into the campaign. The Royal Navy was rather more successful and sunk ten German destroyers, but attention naturally focused on the failure of Anglo-French ground forces in their first major operation of the war. The inquest into this failure led to the fall of the Chamberlain government in May 1940 and its replacement by Churchill's coalition – despite the fact that as First Lord of the Admiralty Churchill had more responsibility than most for the failure in Norway. The new Prime Minister's view of the war differed from that of his predecessor. He sought to galvanise the country for war and worked tirelessly to bring a greater sense of urgency to the war effort, constantly pressing his military commanders to carry the fight to the enemy. But on the day that he came to power his main task was to organise a defensive operation, following the long-awaited German attack in the west on Holland, Belgium and Luxembourg.

It had already been decided that in the event of such an attack, Anglo-French forces would push into the Low Countries in an attempt to hold the Germans. This strategy, though, was obstructed by the refusal of Holland and Belgium to co-ordinate military planning with Britain and France in advance of a German strike, fearing that any such co-operation would be interpreted by Hitler as a breach of neutrality. This lack of Allied planning assisted German forces which had already demonstrated their prowess at short, mobile and highly concentrated campaigns. Motorised divisions, some 2,000 panzer tanks and over 100 infantry divisions were deployed by the Germans in their attack on the west. The close co-ordination between these ground forces and the Luftwaffe meant that firepower was maximised, providing a crucial advantage over the western Allies whose combined forces were at least equal on paper to those of the enemy but who failed to organise their resources in the most effective way. Without a coherent command structure to ensure that troops and equipment were positioned in the right place at the right time, and unable to cope with the speed or direction of the German attacks, Allied forces were overrun. The Low Countries struggled even to slow the invaders. Meanwhile German panzers rolling into France drove a corridor between the British, French and Belgian forces in the north and the remaining French armies in the south. By 20 May the spearhead of the German column had reached the Channel ports, a feat which had eluded the Kaiser's army throughout the 1914–18 war. With the position in France now hopeless, the priority for Britain was the defence of the home islands. This required an evacuation of forces from the continent, so that a sizeable army would be available alongside the RAF and the Royal Navy to resist invasion. As hopes of a French recovery faded and the bulk of the British Expeditionary Force remained trapped at Dunkirk, Britain faced a future as the only European power left in the war against Hitler.

As this crisis developed – and despite Churchill's claims to the contrary – the war cabinet did discuss the possibility of a negotiated settlement with Germany in a series of five long meetings held on 26–8 May. After arguing for so long that war against a combination of Germany, Japan and Italy would be disastrous, Chamberlain and Halifax at least received a vindication of sorts as it became ever more apparent that Britain was struggling to cope in a contest with Germany alone. During the war cabinet meetings in May, both men argued that Mussolini could be approached to act as an intermediary with a brief to explore a possible peace deal; this was supported by the French, for whom a settlement was obviously preferable to the complete military defeat which loomed. Neither Chamberlain nor Halifax advocated peace at any price; a settlement would have to guarantee Britain's independence and ideally the restoration of independence to the Low Countries and France. Assuming that the real purpose of Hitler's attack on the west was to secure that flank in preparation for the invasion of the Soviet Union, it seemed reasonable to believe that acceptable terms could be agreed. Halifax argued with some force that it made sense at least to enquire about such terms via Mussolini – the Allied military position was desperately weak and there was every prospect that Germany would use the airfields and industrial resources it had captured in the west in an attempt to bomb the British into submission. The Foreign Secretary attempted to persuade Churchill that a simple refusal to countenance a settlement could only end in carnage, but the Prime Minister eventually carried the cabinet against Halifax, assisted by a report from the Chiefs of Staff which argued that while Germany enjoyed crucial advantages, the strength of the Royal Navy and the RAF and the morale of the civil population would enable Britain to resist invasion. The case for an early compromise peace was also weakened by the knowledge on 28 May that large numbers of troops would be evacuated from the continent back to Britain.

Reynolds argued that Churchill's stance in these debates was more complex than the simple defiance of legend. He maintained that Churchill was prepared to consider a settlement with Germany, but he judged May 1940 to be the wrong time to conduct discussions (Reynolds 1985: 152–3). In exchanges with Halifax, for example, Churchill said that he would at least consider peace terms if they were offered by Germany after the defeat of France. He even suggested that he would be prepared to surrender territory within the empire as part of a settlement which safeguarded Britain's independence and which saw the Germans concede their overlordship of central Europe. However, he made it clear that he was far less optimistic than Halifax about the possibility of Germany offering peace terms which might prove acceptable. Also, he firmly opposed the idea that Britain should seek a settlement, primarily because it would damage morale at home, but also because it would be interpreted by Hitler and Mussolini as an admission of weakness which would only encourage them to press for exorbitant terms.

There is a danger, though, that Reynold's interpretation of Churchill's position fails to take sufficient account of political context. The war cabinet discussions came less than three weeks after Churchill's elevation to the premiership. As Prime Minister he relied for some time on the continued support of colleagues who had been the architects of appeasement – Chamberlain, who remained the Conservative Party leader, and Halifax, who remained Foreign Secretary and who had been the choice of many as Prime Minister after the Norway debate. Churchill was therefore anxious to avoid alienating either of his colleagues and risk their resignation from the cabinet. In the discussions about a negotiated settlement, Churchill was forced to argue his case with some care and to adopt at times a conciliatory position. By arguing that Britain's negotiating position in future peace talks would be strengthened by remaining in the war at least until an attempted German invasion had been repelled, Churchill was able to achieve his main objective of continuing the conflict, but in a way that appeared to leave the door open for a settlement, perhaps within a few months, thereby retaining the support of Chamberlain and Halifax. Arguably the real views of Churchill were expressed at a meeting with ministers outside of the war cabinet on 28 May, during which he proclaimed his determination to fight to the finish. Hugh Dalton recorded the meeting in his diary:

> Therefore, [Churchill] said, 'We shall go on and we shall fight it out, here or elsewhere, and if at last the long story is to end, it were better it should end, not through surrender, but only when we are rolling senseless on the ground.' There was a murmer of approval round the table, in which I think Amery, Lord Lloyd and I were loudest. Not much more was said. No one expressed even the faintest flicker of dissent.
>
> (Pimlott 1986: 29)

It was a performance charged with typical Churchillian rhetoric, designed in part to rally government morale, but in all probability it sprang from a deeply held conviction that negotiations with the Nazi regime were strategically and morally unacceptable.

Britain alone, June 1940–June 1941

As Britain prepared for the struggle ahead the last days of the defeat of France were played out. Mussolini led Italy into war against a French nation on the verge of defeat on 10 June, anxious to share in the division of any territory. With French defences breached in almost every part of the country, the new government of Marshal Pétain sought and obtained an armistice with Germany and Italy which took effect on 25 June. The north and west of France were occupied by German troops, the south-east territory which bordered Italy was occupied by Mussolini's forces, but the remainder of the country was controlled by a French government seated at Vichy and the French empire was not disturbed. The armistice broke the Anglo-French agreement that neither would make a separate peace with Germany and there was intense frustration in Britain that the French had decided against continuing the war from north Africa. With the Germans in control of the French Atlantic ports, with the possibility that the French fleet would be deployed by Germany against the Royal Navy and with French economic and industrial resources now in enemy hands, Churchill's attention turned fully to Britain's defence. The most immediate concern was the fate of the French fleet which, under the terms of the armistice, was to be disarmed under German or Italian supervision. Unwilling to risk the seizure of French vessels by the Germans, and after claiming that satisfactory assurances from France about the fate of their ships had not been secured, British warships attacked the French on 3 July 1940 at Mers-el-Kebir in north Africa. It was a highly controversial decision, causing the death of 1,300 French seamen, and it was railroaded through by Churchill against the scepticism of cabinet colleagues and the Admiralty. Anglo-French relations were seriously damaged, a factor which later hindered British attempts to secure French co-operation against the Axis powers. In harsh political terms, though, the cost of alienating a defeated France was offset by the benefit of proving to the United States that Britain was determined to continue the war until the end. Churchill in particular believed that Britain had to show it was worthy of American support. The economic and material assistance of the United States was vital to Britain's survival; better still, if it could be persuaded to enter the war on Britain's side the prospects of victory would be transformed.

In the meantime the attack at Mers-el-Kebir had helped to prevent a decisive tilt in the naval balance against Britain in the Atlantic and Mediterranean. This strengthened its defences against the attempted invasion of the home islands which was expected in the summer of 1940. Before a sea-borne invasion was launched, though, the battle for air supremacy had to be waged. Hitler had instructed the Luftwaffe, which now operated from bases in France and Belgium, that their task was to achieve control of the skies, smash coastal defences and break the resistance of enemy land forces. In one of the most heroic episodes of Britain's war effort the RAF, helped by radar communication and the high output of aircraft from the factories of Vickers and Hawker, prevented the Germans from dominating the skies. The resistance of Fighter Command has a rightful place in the roll-call of British military triumphs, but this should not disguise the fact that the outcome of the Battle of Britain owed as much to German strategic errors as it did to the valour and skill of RAF pilots. For example, only in late August did the Luftwaffe successfully concentrate their forces in pursuit of a clear objective: the destruction of RAF fighter airfields in south-east England and the sector-stations which directed operations. By early September the strategy had begun to provide the Germans with a clear advantage in the battle. At this point it made sense for the Luftwaffe to continue the attacks on airfields and to combine them with raids on aircraft factories and radar installations. But on 7 September the attack was switched to London; perhaps in an attempt to bring the air battle to an earlier conclusion (Keegan 1997: 79); perhaps because the Luftwaffe believed they had crippled the front-line squadrons of Fighter Command and now only needed to engage in open combat the reserve squadrons, which they were sure would be deployed to defend the capital (Parker 1990: 50). Civilians in London paid a heavy price for this decision, but crucially it gave Fighter Command time to repair its forward airfields and regroup in sufficient strength to inflict heavy losses on the German bombers which raided London. After missing the opportunity to gain control of the skies Hitler postponed his invasion plans on 17 September. As autumn set in and weather conditions made a cross-Channel operation impossible, Hitler was forced to concede on 12 October that invasion was ruled out at least until spring 1941.

Churchill knew from intelligence intercepts that Britain was safe from invasion for a time. The threat to the empire, however, remained and almost immediately the focus of the war effort moved to the defence of Britain's position in the Middle East and Mediterranean – a reordering of priorities which was to have profound consequences for the future direction of British and later Allied strategy. The initiative in the region was taken by the Italians who attacked British forces in Egypt on 13 September 1940. Although the aggression was hardly welcome, it came in an ideal place for Britain's armies to make a stand because General Wavell's forces were already positioned in the region. After a series of unsuccessful encounters with the Germans, there was a good chance that Wavell would be able to secure a morale-boosting victory against the less powerful Italians in north Africa. British control of the southern seaboard of the eastern Mediterranean would also bring obvious strategic advantages: sea communication between Egypt and

India would be kept open; oil supplies in the Middle East would be protected for Britain and denied to the enemy; and if defeats were inflicted on the Italians in the desert there was every chance that the Germans would be drawn reluctantly into north Africa to support their ally.

Ignoring almost constant pressure from Churchill to launch an offensive, Wavell's initial response to the Italian advance was to retreat, inflict maximum casualties on the enemy and wait for the moment to counter attack. Wavell was determined to ensure that his troops were properly trained and equipped before they made their move against Italian forces which enjoyed the advantage of numbers and heavily fortified defences. When the counter attack – codenamed Compass – came on 9 December it achieved results which surpassed even the most optimistic expectations. By February 1941 the Western Desert Force, led by General O'Connor, had advanced 500 miles, routed ten Italian divisions and captured 130,000 prisoners and 400 tanks (Beckett 1992: 77). In the same month General Cunningham opened Britain's campaign in east Africa, attacking Italian Somaliland from Kenya. Despite numerous logistical difficulties the campaign was a success; by May 1941 Mussolini's east African empire had largely been destroyed. Arguably, Britain had an opportunity to concentrate its forces in the region and clear the enemy from north Africa during 1941. It was not taken. Instead, in what has been described as perhaps the boldest strategic decision of the war, troops and equipment were diverted to help Greece in their fight against the Italians and Germans (Keegan 1995: 18). The dispersal of resources was a brave stroke indeed, but it weakened Britain's position in north Africa at a crucial time. German armoured forces, including Erwin Rommel's panzers, poured in and immediately attacked Egypt: for the next two years dominance of north Africa swung like a pendulum between the two opposing forces until Germany was finally forced out of Tunisia in May 1943.

The decision to aid the Greeks at the expense of the campaign in north Africa was motivated primarily by political considerations. Britain had pledged to defend Greece in 1939. As important, though, was the obligation that Britain felt to any nation attacked by enemies against whom it had stood alone since June 1940 – Italy invaded Greece in October 1940 and there were clear signs that Germany was seeking to build on its position in the Balkans. Churchill expressed reservations about action in Greece once it was known that this was likely to involve facing German rather than simply Italian troops, but his doubts were overcome by the combined optimism of Eden, Wavell and the Chiefs of

Staff. Churchill's doubts were to prove well founded. Germany attacked Greece on 6 April 1941 and soon overwhelmed both Greek and British opposition – a simultaneous attack on Yugoslavia strengthened still further Germany's hand. In addition to enjoying air supremacy, the Germans were able to supply their forces over land routes; the British in contrast relied on the navy for the movement of troops and equipment, a process hampered by German disruption of shipping through the Suez Canal. By 29 April the bulk of the British force had been evacuated from Greece, minus its equipment as at Dunkirk. Some 20,000 troops were taken to Crete, but the respite was temporary. Inadequate preparation left the defences of Crete powerless against the Luftwaffe, now operating from the Greek mainland. On 20 May German planes and paratroopers launched an airborne assault and by the end of the month Crete too was lost. It was the end of a disastrous few months for Britain, compounded by the early successes of Rommel's Africa Corps against a depleted British force which now began to concede the ground it had won in late 1940 and early 1941.

From a British perspective, the one sign of light amidst the gloom was the evidence that Germany was preparing to attack the Soviet Union, a strike which would provide enormous relief to Britain. Tension between the two partners in the Nazi–Soviet pact had been increasing markedly since August 1939, despite co-operation in a number of spheres. There were notable disagreements over policy towards Finland, Romania and Hungary. When German troops occupied Bulgaria, ostensibly as a base for their attack on Greece, the Soviets protested that it violated their own security interests. They had a point: the occupation of Bulgaria can be seen primarily as preparation for Hitler's long-intended attack on the Soviet Union (Weinberg 1994: 202). The Nazi–Soviet pact had bought valuable time for the Germans, time in which they consolidated their position on the continent, knocked France out of the war and built up their military forces in advance of their major campaign in the east. By late May 1941 intelligence confirmed that a large German army was massed on the Russian frontier. On 21 June this force smashed into Soviet territory in an operation codenamed Barbarossa. As the tanks rolled eastwards Britain was faced with some hard strategic choices.

Towards the Grand Alliance, June– December 1941

Churchill's offer of full support to the Soviet Union was broadcast on 22 June. In the short term this involved diverting supplies to the east and issuing a joint Declaration with Russia which promised mutual help and a guarantee that neither partner would make a separate peace. In August the two powers co-operated in military action in Persia, now called Iran. By December the new solidarity had developed further as Britain joined the Soviets in their war against Finland, Romania and Hungary. Churchill regretted the break with the Finns in particular, but saw it as a price worth paying to a major ally in the war against Hitler; it was also a valuable way of appeasing Stalin who was calling in vain for the British to open up a second front in western Europe.

After a year in which Britain had been the only European power in the war against Germany Churchill's enthusiasm for Anglo-Soviet co-operation was understandable. Historians, though, have recently questioned the wisdom of British policy before and after Barbarossa. According to John Charmley, Churchill was too quick to throw unequivocal support, supplies and diplomatic concessions at Russia at a time when they had been forced into the war and the pressure was off Britain. A more serious charge is that by focusing so intently on the defeat of Hitler, Churchill failed to consider how co-operation with the Soviets would affect the balance of power in Europe in the longer term. Britain fought to counter the threat of German dominance on the continent, but in the process it helped to bring about Soviet dominance in Europe; moreover, Britain emerged from the conflict almost bankrupt, over-reliant on the support of the United States, and with its grip on the empire severely weakened (Charmley 1993: 456, 467, 590, 604–8, 648–9). Charmley's revisionist text at no point argued that Britain should have withdrawn from the war, but the controversy which greeted his biography of Churchill was intensified by a review written by Alan Clark in *The Times* in 1993. The military historian and former defence minister suggested that Britain should have made peace with Germany in 1941 before the invasion of the Soviet Union. Rudolf Hess, Hitler's deputy, had flown to Britain in May with suggested terms for peace. If Britain had taken advantage of such an offer, argued Clark, the fleet and spitfires could have been moved to Singapore to defend the far eastern empire, British lives would have been saved and the country would have been spared economic exhaustion and the need to rely on the support of the United States. The most serious problem with this counter-factual thesis, though, is that the details of the Hess mission

– made without Hitler's approval – are not known, so there is no certainty that acceptable terms could have been agreed with an enemy which had conquered France and the Low Countries, taken control of the Channel ports and secured territory in the Balkans and north Africa which threatened Britain's imperial lifeline in the Mediterranean.

The reality is that Germany's invasion of the Soviet Union led political and military leaders in Britain to take a more positive view of the war effort, not to seek a route out. The British after all had long understood that they were incapable of defeating Germany on their own. After the surrender of France the strategy was to hold out and hope that a major ally would come to the rescue. In June 1941 such an ally arrived, albeit one that was kicked into war reluctantly. Even though Barbarossa put Russia on the defensive immediately, even though there were doubts about the reliability of Soviet forces following Stalin's purge of the officer class in the 1930s, Britain was now allied with the second most powerful nation in the world, the nation which held the key to the defeat of Germany in the east.

Churchill welcomed this support, but the partnership he longed for above all else was with the United States. From the outset as First Lord of the Admiralty and then as Prime Minister he corresponded regularly with the US President Roosevelt and attempted to convince him that America should enter the war. Churchill believed that the cultural ties between the two nations would lead to a groundswell of popular support for Britain's war effort in the US, particularly once German air attacks began on British cities. In the crisis of May 1940 he attempted to pressurise the US out of its neutrality, informing Roosevelt that if Britain was forced to the point of collapse it might legitimately use its fleet as a bargaining counter with the Germans. At a time when the 'one-ocean' US navy was guarding against Japan in the Pacific, this threat played on US fears that Hitler could gain control of the Atlantic east coast of America (Reynolds 1985: 162–5).

For all Churchill's efforts, though, the US position before Pearl Harbor was to assist Britain in all ways short of war – the fact that such assistance usually brought the maximum strategic and commercial advantage to the United States also caused some resentment in Britain. It was noted for instance that large-scale purchases of weapons and supplies by Britain provided much needed capital for the US defence industries. In the summer of 1940 Britain allowed the US to site naval bases on British territories in the Caribbean and western Atlantic on long leases in exchange for fifty American destroyers of first world war vintage and varying states of disrepair. Furthermore, in an attempt to overcome a desperate shortage of foreign exchange, British-owned companies in the US were sold off at below market value. When there were few assets left to liquidate Roosevelt signed the Lend Lease Agreement in March 1941, which meant that Britain would continue to receive US supplies for as long as they were required and the bills would be settled after the war: in all, some $27 billion worth of purchases were received under the scheme, covering 54 per cent of Britain's total payments deficit during the conflict (Reynolds 1991: 152). It is difficult to over-estimate the importance of this agreement to Britain's war effort, but of course it came at a price. In return for Lend Lease the US demanded free and equal access to the markets of Britain's empire, the elimination of imperial preference and the abolition of sterling controls. These commercial priorities – which spelt out that the US had no interest in helping Britain to defend and maintain its empire – were also written into the Atlantic Charter, the declaration of Anglo-American aims for the post-war world which was issued in August 1941.

Despite the concessions Britain made in pursuit of an Anglo-American alliance, it was the Japanese attack on Pearl Harbor on 7 December 1941 which finally brought the United States into the war; fortunately for Britain Hitler declared war on the US four days later and ensured that the Americans would fight in Europe as well as in the Pacific. After hearing of the Japanese strike, Churchill declared that Britain was now saved. The United States had joined Britain and Russia in the contest against Germany, Italy and Japan – the Axis powers – and their minor partners. The Grand Alliance at last was in place.

The Mediterranean strategy, 1942–4

As Soviet forces continued to defend their home soil, the new alliance of Britain and America had already made its first major strategic decision. The defeat of Germany would take priority over Japan, because Germany was the most powerful of the Axis partners and the bulk of Allied forces could be deployed against it simultaneously. There was less agreement, however, about the best way to defeat Germany. Some senior American strategists such as General Marshall, the US Army Chief of Staff, argued for an Allied invasion of north-west Europe at the first feasible opportunity: in practice this meant some time in 1943, with a contingency plan for an emergency invasion in late 1942 if the Russians seemed likely to collapse. In March 1942 Marshall explained his reasoning in a memorandum to Roosevelt: the Allies should concentrate on western Europe because England could be used as a base in which to build up manpower; England had airfields which would make it possible for the Allies to achieve air superiority over the battlefield; it made no sense to risk the transfer of British forces overseas in preparation for an attack in a region other than western Europe; and a cross-Channel invasion would provide the maximum support to the Soviets. Following the advice of the nineteenth-century German military strategist Clausewitz that the best way to defeat an enemy was to attack at its heart, Marshall argued that Allied action elsewhere would be nothing more than a 'side-show'.

Churchill and the British Chiefs of Staff held a different view. Given the success of the Germans by 1942 there was understandable reluctance to commit British troops to an early invasion of north-west Europe, a region which stirred memories of the stalemate and carnage of the first world war. Because it would take time for US forces to mobilise fully, the main responsibility for an invasion even in early 1943 would have fallen on Britain; the harsh truth was that the record of defeats in Norway, France, the Balkans, north Africa and more recently against Japan in the Far East did not inspire confidence in the ability of British forces to carry out such a difficult operation. To attempt a cross-Channel invasion and fail would be disastrous, most likely it would set the Allied war effort back several years. There were two factors in particular which heightened the chances of failure. First, although the Allies could in theory gain air superiority given time, control of the skies over north-west Europe remained in the hands of the Germans in 1942. Second, German control of the French Atlantic ports had enabled Admiral Dönitz to extend his U-boat operations further west into the Atlantic, successfully attacking convoys and seriously disrupting the movement of supplies to Britain. Realising the importance of the Battle of the Atlantic, Hitler increased the construction of the U-boat fleet in late 1941 – perhaps in retrospect too late – until there were 300 vessels by July 1942. Throughout 1941 these U-boats had sunk some 1,200 ships, a tonnage of over 4 million; with more U-boats operational in 1942 they sunk over 1,600 ships, a tonnage of almost 8 million. According to British strategists, such losses and the continued threat of the U-boats ruled out an early invasion of north-west Europe. In any case, it was added, the Soviets had proven themselves capable of holding out against the Germans without the help of a second front in the west; and Britain and the US could carry the fight to Germany with the use of strategic bombing.

Both Churchill and Roosevelt appreciated that it would take time to prepare an Anglo-US force which could invade France in sufficient strength to minimise the dangers of failure. But they also agreed that some joint operation had to be undertaken in 1942. In the first place, there was pressure to respond to Soviet pleas for assistance at a time when there was widespread public sympathy for Russia, particularly in Britain. This was accompanied by the misplaced fear that the Russians would make a separate peace with Hitler if the western Allies failed to provide some relief. Second, if America did not involve itself in action against Germany and Italy in 1942, there was a danger that US public opinion and the Pacific lobby in Washington would demand a massive transfer of resources to the war against Japan, thereby undermining the 'Germany first' strategy. Throughout the spring and summer of 1942 Churchill continued to resist all the US and Soviet arguments for a cross-Channel operation; instead he pushed for an attack on the Axis powers in north Africa, a plan which contradicted the wishes of his Chiefs of Staff but which Roosevelt nevertheless accepted. Plans were therefore drawn up for an Anglo-American invasion of north Africa – codenamed Operation Torch.

There were several reasons why Torch was adopted. It followed Britain's traditional strategy of using seapower to stretch a continental enemy's lines of communication by attacking along an exposed coastline. Landings in north Africa would meet with less resistance than a similar operation against well-defended positions in France – it was also an advantage here that the bulk of Axis forces in north Africa were Italian not German. American troops would be given their first experience of battle in the west in a context in which defeats would be a setback rather than a disaster: valuable lessons would be learned about training, equipment, tactics and command (Weinberg 1994: 437). Also as Churchill explained to Stalin, who was disappointed at the failure of the western Allies to open a second front in France, Allied control of the north-African seaboard would make possible an invasion of Europe across the Mediterranean, through Italy and the Balkans. Churchill's vision was of a ring tightening on Germany, with Allied forces eventually advancing from the east, south and north. In the meantime, Torch would at least draw some German firepower away from the Soviets in the east. There was some suspicion in America and Russia that the British were seeking to delay a cross-Channel invasion in favour of an operation which would safeguard their interests in Egypt, Suez and the oil-rich territories of the Middle East. But this ignores the simple fact that the bulk of Britain's land forces were in the western desert anyway – in that sense north Africa was an obvious theatre for an Allied offensive. Also, the ever-optimistic Churchill did not believe that Torch would rule out the chances of an Allied invasion of France in 1943.

In November 1942 Anglo-US forces under the command of the American General Eisenhower made three separate landings in Vichy-controlled French north Africa: at Oran and Tangiers in Algeria and at Casablanca in Morocco. Initially the landings met fierce resistance from the French – with memories of Mers-el-Kebir still alive – but hurried diplomacy, good fortune and the arrival of Allied troops in large numbers helped to ensure that opposition soon turned to co-operation. Churchill's argument that troops should have landed further east towards Tunisia at the beginning of the operation was ignored by the Americans; as a result, by the time the Allies had driven the 500 miles from Algiers to Tunis the Germans had poured in reinforcements and were able to hold out for months, frustrating Allied hopes that north Africa could be cleared in a matter of weeks. The landings in north-west Africa, therefore, were only a partial success, but the boost they gave to morale was heightened by the fact that they came just a few days after the victory of Montgomery's Eighth Army further east in Egypt at El Alamein: the first major defeat of the Germans by the British on land. Together with the more significant development of the Russian counter-offensive at Stalingrad, the victories helped to establish late 1942 as the 'turn of the tide' in the war: from this point on the Grand Alliance was on the offensive.

In January 1943 Roosevelt and Churchill met at the Casablanca conference to discuss strategy after Torch. It was here, according to Grigg, that a series of mistakes was made which delayed the cross-Channel invasion by a year and prolonged the war unnecessarily. For instance, it was decided at Casablanca that priority should be given to driving the Germans out of Tunis; Grigg argued that this took up valuable time when the Germans could have been contained in Tunis and simply left to rot (Grigg 1985: 82). Next, it was agreed that once north Africa was secured the invasion of Sicily and mainland Italy would follow; Grigg implied that this was a waste of resources and pointed out that the Allied armada used in the invasion of Sicily in 1943 was larger than the one which set sail for Normandy in 1944 – in short, an invasion of France rather than Italy would have been possible in 1943 if Allied leaders had shown the will (Grigg 1985: 218–19). Next, it was agreed that the Allies would seek the unconditional surrender of the enemy; Grigg complained that this restricted the freedom of the Allies to secure an early settlement and discouraged peace-inclined elements on the other side. He blamed the policy for the delay in negotiating an armistice with Italy in 1943 and claimed that it provided a gift to the German propaganda machine (Grigg 1985: 77–8).

The way in which the Mediterranean strategy unfolded certainly ruled out an invasion of France until 1944. After Tunisia was finally captured in May 1943 the invasion of the island of Sicily followed in July. Within days of the invasion Mussolini's fascist regime collapsed, but the Italian surrender did not come until September when the Allies crossed to the mainland. Their progress here was slower than expected: partly because of an impressive rearguard action by the Germans; partly because the mountainous Italian terrain suited defensive rather than offensive action; and partly because of the failure of British and American commanders to work together effectively. Although Churchill referred to the Italian peninsular as the 'soft underbelly' of the Axis in Europe, it was in Italy that the British and Americans fought their toughest battles against the Germans on any front during the war (Keegan 1997: 295). Rome was not taken until May 1944 and the Germans continued to defend northern Italy throughout the winter.

Stalin protested about the decision to invade Italy in 1943 and the consequent postponement of the second front in western Europe. His protest was in part based on military considerations: the delay meant that Russia's repeated calls for assistance in the west were ignored for three years. But it was also motivated by political considerations: Stalin calculated that he could win diplomatic concessions from Britain and America by constantly complaining about their failure to provide military assistance in western Europe. The tactic appeared to bring rewards. For example, at the Teheran conference in late 1943 it was agreed that the Soviets could keep the Polish territory which they had taken in 1939; at Moscow in 1944 Churchill indicated that he was prepared to accept a strong Soviet presence in the Balkans after the war. These concessions of course reflected the fact that the Soviets would eventually control territories in Europe which they had no intention of leaving – the irony here was that Churchill used the same practical justifications for appeasing Stalin that Chamberlain had used before with Hitler. But for those historians who argue that an invasion of France could have succeeded in 1943, the decision to delay the Normandy landings until 1944 needlessly consolidated Russia's hold on eastern Europe, an outcome which had profound consequences for the post-war world. The delay gave the Soviets more time to advance westwards, capturing territory and eventually meeting their western

Allies in Germany rather than further east. It also damaged diplomatic relations between the western Allies and the Soviets, whose Red Army was left with the main burden of fighting the Germans for three years.

It is difficult to resist the claim that a successful invasion of France in 1943 would have brought considerable advantages to the western Allies and spared parts of eastern Europe decades of Soviet dominance. Arguably too it would have hastened the end of the war, spared many lives and saved large numbers of Jews in the Nazi camps. The problem of course lies in supporting the assumption that an invasion in 1943 would have succeeded. In its favour is the argument that the Germans were in a weaker position to resist invasion in 1943 than they were a year later: Hitler's coastal defence of northern Europe – the Atlantic Wall – was not yet complete; German divisions in France were under strength and short of vital equipment; and Hitler's forces were struggling in Russia, further away from France than they were in 1944 (Keegan 1995: 21; Lamb 1993: 344). However, from the vantage point of strategists at the time there were good reasons to exercise caution: the U-boat menace, which hampered the build-up of an invasion force in Britain, was not cleared from the Atlantic until May 1943; in the first quarter of 1943 the shipping of US troops abroad was behind schedule (Parker 1990: 125); there was limited time available to assemble sufficient landing craft, train troops and produce the required supplies; and there was understandable reluctance to risk the lives of so many troops in a massive operation when there were doubts about its feasibility – this much at least had been learned from the first world war. The debate about 1943 versus 1944 will perhaps never be settled: all we know for sure is that the British won the argument at the time and the Allied invasion of France was delayed until June 1944.

D-Day and victory in Europe

By the end of 1943 the US had mobilised sufficient armed forces to make them the senior partner in the Anglo-American relationship. The result was a US timetable and Commander – General Eisenhower – for the D-Day landings in 1944, codenamed Overlord. The invasion of Normandy began on 6 June 1944, following a massive preliminary bombardment from air and sea. The bulk of the assault troops were carried in more than 4,000 landing craft to five beachheads – Utah, Omaha, Gold, Juno and Sword – all of which were controlled by the Allies at the end of D-Day. The main difficulties were experienced by the US First Infantry Division, which took several hours to push its way off Omaha beach, defended by the best German formation in a coastal position on D-Day (Keegan 1997: 322). Although the Allies were unable to link up their five beachheads into a continuous front until 12 June, casualties were lower than expected and crucially the Germans failed to push any of the Allied armies back into the sea. In part this was because Hitler thought until late that the Normandy landings were a diversion in advance of a main Allied invasion of the Pas de Calais region. An elaborate deception plan, involving a fictitious US First Army Group supposedly based in Kent and Sussex, led the Germans to conclude that the Allies would cross the Channel at its narrowest point (Howard 1992: 119–22). As a result the largest German army in the west was held back from Normandy until August to meet an attack which never came.

The Germans' initial advantage of men and material on the battle-field was lost as the Allies won the race to build up troop numbers, helped by the use of floating mulberry harbours which had been towed across the Channel, the capture of the port of Cherbourg on 26 June and air superiority of seventy to one. By 5 July one million Allied troops had landed in Normandy, faced by some 400,000 German defenders whose only hope now was to slow rather than repel the enemy. To make matters worse, the Germans also had to face a Soviet offensive in the east which began on 22 June and which inflicted on the German army its biggest defeat of the war. This was the prelude to a massive summer offensive by the Soviets, crossing their pre-war borders and sweeping towards Warsaw, Bucharest and Sofia. Between June and September 1944 the German army in the east lost 215,000 killed and 625,000 missing; the comparable German losses in the west were 55,000 killed and 340,000 missing (Parker 1990: 209).

Given the success of the Normandy landings and the scale of German casualties by late summer 1944, the obvious question is why victory in Europe was delayed until May 1945. To a large extent the prolongation of the war reflected the determination of Nazi leaders to fight to the death rather than surrender, not least because victors' justice would demand the execution of prominent Nazis anyway. Hitler also believed that if the conflict could be dragged out for as long as possible one of the partners in the Grand Alliance might be persuaded to sign a separate peace. Britain perhaps offered the best hopes of a compromise, particularly as it was vulnerable to the Germans' new secret weapons – the V-1 flying bomb, the first of which arrived in June 1944, and the V-2 rocket, which was used from September 1944 mainly against London and the Allies' logistic base in Antwerp. Goebbels's

Ministry of Propaganda exploited the impact of these new weapons, giving the German people some confidence that the war was not necessarily lost, despite the pressure of the Allied advances from east and west.

The resolve of the Germans to continue the fight against over-whelming odds was also stiffened by the enemy's insistence on unconditional surrender and the announcement of tough Allied plans for post-war Germany. Lamb argued that the commitment to unconditional surrender was an error of judgement which delayed the end of the war (Lamb 1993: 286–99). It may have served some purpose when it was announced in 1943, reassuring Stalin that the western Allies had no intention of making a separate peace, but it offered no encouragement to dissident or peace-inclined elements in Germany who saw little point in continuing the war in the west after Anglo-US forces had invaded France in 1944 – Rommel, Beck and other German Generals wished to conclude an armistice in the west and switch their forces to the east to help keep the Soviets out of Germany. Churchill, though, was adamant that nothing short of unconditional surrender could be offered, even if an anti-Nazi government was formed in Germany. This was a severe blow to the German opposition, which included army officers, politicians, trade union leaders and bishops from the Protestant and Catholic churches; they were prepared to move against the Nazi leadership and to accept a peace which involved reparations and the withdrawal of all German forces from occupied territories, but they could never accept unconditional surrender without inviting the charge that they had betrayed the country's fighting forces. Churchill refused to take this German opposition seriously, even after the Stauffenberg bomb plot of 20 July 1944 which almost killed Hitler. He also refused to listen to Eisenhower's observation that the insistence on unconditional surrender – renamed by Goebbels as 'total slavery' – helped to maintain the morale of German forces in autumn 1944 and prolong the war.

Germany's determination to resist unconditional surrender was intensified by the announcement of the Morgenthau Plan in September 1944. This stated that the Allies intended to convert post-war Germany into a primarily pastoral and agricultural country, with the metallurgi-cal, chemical and electrical industries on the Ruhr and the Saar closed down to prevent the build-up of a war machine in future. Goebbels claimed that the Allies wanted to starve the German people; he also made useful propaganda out of Allied plans to transfer land to the Soviet Union and Poland after the war and to expel millions of

Germans from their homes in the east. Faced with the apparent prospect of brutal treatment after defeat, many of Hitler's armies – now frequently made up of teenagers, older men, injured troops and others combed out of every possible source – fought tenaciously in the west through 1944. In August they launched a counter-offensive at Mortain, known as the Battle of the Falaise Gap, which developed into the largest clash of armour fought on the western front. It lasted for two weeks before the Germans withdrew in the face of massive Allied air-power.

Despite heavy losses, the Germans launched another counter-attack in December through the Ardennes. Unlike their successful attack in 1940 the Germans were slowed by shortages of transport and fuel; they also ran into a fierce defensive operation from US troops who were able to call up motorised reinforcements quickly and who were supported from the air. The attack was halted on 25 December and by the middle of January the battle was effectively over: the Germans had lost 100,000 men, 800 tanks and 1,000 aircraft (Keegan 1997: 371). Losses of this scale could not be sustained, particularly against Allied forces which seemed to have a limitless supply of US troops and material. The Ardennes assault was Hitler's last gamble and it failed. It delayed the Allied advance, but the cost was massive and it weakened Germany's eastern front at a crucial time. As the Allies closed in on Berlin from either direction in 1945, determined rearguard actions by the Germans slowed their progress; arguably, too, if there had been less rivalry between Montgomery on the British side and Eisenhower, Patton and Bradley on the US side, then the western Allies would have reached Berlin sooner. But no amount of German resolve or Anglo-US wrangling could change the outcome of the war. On 30 April Hitler committed suicide in Berlin; on 7 May at Eisenhower's headquarters at Reims the unconditional surrender of Germany was received by representatives of Britain, France, USA and USSR; 'VE Day' was celebrated in Britain and America the next day. The war in the east continued until the following August when two atomic bombs were dropped on the Japanese cities of Hiroshima and Nagasaki: it was with a perverse logic that the most violent conflict the world had known ended with history's most violent single acts.

Conclusion

Ultimately it was US and Soviet power which won the war, but Britain played a crucial part, especially between the summers of 1940 and 1941 when it stood alone in Europe and helped to define the moral nature of the contest. True, the Grand Alliance had economic, material and manpower advantages over the enemy which proved irresistible, particularly after the Normandy landings. Probably the most crucial advantage of all for the Allies was air supremacy in the west: British and American aircraft pounded German cities day and night, drew air cover away from the German army in the east and ensured Allied success after the invasion of France in 1944. But to secure victory such advantages had to be accompanied by a strong conviction that the hardship and sacrifice of war were worth bearing – for citizens as well as soldiers. The belief in the cause and the determination to succeed helped each member of the Grand Alliance to learn the lessons of early setbacks and to come back stronger and better prepared; it helped the Red Army to pull back from the brink of collapse, hold out at Stalingrad and eventually push the Germans back the long haul to Berlin; it helped to underpin the US production effort and to sustain US troops fighting thousands of miles away from home; and it helped the British to recover from a sequence of defeats between 1940 and 1942 (Overy 1996: 314–25).

Although victory was secured, criticisms have been made of British and Allied strategy: the failure to attack Germany at the start of the war; the decision to switch troops from north Africa to Greece in 1941; the rejection of an opportunity to explore a compromise peace before Hitler invaded the Soviet Union; the selection and handling of a Mediterranean strategy in 1942 and 1943; the delay in the invasion of France until 1944; the commitment to unconditional surrender and the announcement of tough plans for post-war Germany. These criticisms make for interesting debate, but for the most part they rely on counter-factual hypothesising – we simply cannot know what would have happened if different strategic decisions had been made during the war.

There is no question that after six years of war the price of victory was high. Britain lost 264,000 servicemen and 90,000 civilians, plus more than 100,000 dead in the empire – not counting the millions of Indians who died in the famine of 1943 (Parker 1990: 285). The empire was left vulnerable both to the internal forces of nationalism and US demands that Britain scale down its imperial commitments, but these pressures had been present even before 1939 and it is difficult to accept the claim that a different handling of wartime strategy would have saved the empire in the longer term. The strain of supplying the war effort left the country's industry and economy exhausted and debt-ridden; by 1945 Britain was reliant on Washington for economic and strategic support and its future place in the world was as a junior partner of the US. In that sense, victory did not secure Britain's independence. Neither did it secure a balance of power on the continent, because at the end of the conflict the Soviets were left dominant in eastern Europe – almost immediately world war was replaced by cold war between east and west.

In the final analysis, though, the price was surely worth paying. The defeat of German and Italian fascist states and the surrender of imperial Japan were worthy objectives to pursue to the end: an alternative conclusion to the war would have been disastrous. For Britain, much of Europe and the wider world the defeat of the Axis powers meant a safer and more civilised future. Of course some – including Britain – faced a better future than others. In post-war western Europe the US Marshall Plan provided aid which helped to rebuild industry and infrastructure and ease the cost of welfare programmes. The creation of the North Atlantic Treaty Organisation (NATO) in 1949 signalled the willingness of the US to underwrite the security of the west. Meanwhile, nations in western Europe began the move towards economic and political integration which led to the Treaty of Rome in 1957. Britain eventually recognised that its future lay in the European Economic Community (EEC) rather than the empire, but still it retained some of the important trappings of world power status – such as a permanent seat on the Security Council of the United Nations. Most important of all, after two major wars in the first half of the twentieth century, Britain and France stood alongside a democratic West Germany in NATO by 1954. Co-operation was taken still further in 1973 when the three became partners in the EEC: friction and quarrels lay ahead in the new European structures, but war was consigned to the past.

Bibliography

For ease of reference the bibliography has been organised thematically. In cases where an item is relevant to more than one section it appears under the heading where it has been used most frequently in the text.

General

Beloff, M. (1984) *Wars and Welfare: Britain 1914–45*, London: Edward Arnold.

Bosworth, R. J. B. (1993) *Explaining Auschwitz and Hiroshima: History Writing and the Second World War 1945–1990*, London: Routledge.

Calvocoressi, P. and Wint, G. (1972) *Total War*, London: Allen Lane.

Mowat, C. L. (1955) *Britain Between the Wars*, London: Methuen.

Pelling, H. (1970) *Britain and the Second World War*, London: Fontana.

Reynolds, D., Kimball, W. and Chubarian A. O. (eds) (1994) *Allies at War*, London: Macmillan.

Taylor, A. J. P. (1965) *English History 1914–1945*, Oxford: Oxford University Press.

Politics and society

Addison, P. (1973) 'By-elections of the second world war', in C. Cook and J. Ramsden (eds) *By-elections in British Politics*, London: Macmillan.

—— (1975) *The Road to 1945: British Politics and the Second World War*, London: Jonathan Cape.

—— (1992) *Churchill on the Home Front 1900–1955*, London: Jonathan Cape.

—— (1997) 'Churchill and the price of victory: 1939–1945', in N. Tiratsoo (ed.) *From Blitz to Blair: A New History of Britain since 1939*, London: Weidenfeld and Nicolson.

Baines, M. (1995) 'The Liberal party and the 1945 general election', *Contemporary Record*, 9, 1: 48–61.

Baldwin, P. (1990) *The Politics of Social Solidarity: Class Bases of the European Welfare State 1875–1975*, Cambridge: Cambridge University Press.

Blake, R. (1996) 'How Churchill became Prime Minister', in R. Blake and Wm. Roger Louis (eds) *Churchill*, Oxford: Clarendon Press.

Braybon, G. and Summerfield, P. (1987) *Out of the Cage: Women's Experiences in Two World Wars*, London: Pandora Press.

Brooke, S. (1992) *Labour's War: The Labour Party During the Second World War*, Oxford: Oxford University Press.

—— (1995) 'The Labour party and the 1945 general election', *Contemporary Record*, 9, 1: 1–21.

Bullock, A. (1967) *The Life and Times of Ernest Bevin*, Vol. II, *Minister of Labour 1940–5*, London: Heinemann.

Burgess, S. (1991) '1945 observed: a history of the histories', *Contemporary Record*, 5, 1: 155–70.

Calder, A. (1992 edn) *The People's War: Britain 1939–1945*, London: Pimlico.

Calder, A. and Sheridan, D. (eds) (1984) *Speak for Yourself: A Mass-Observation Anthology 1937–1949*, Oxford: Oxford University Press.

Callaghan, J. (1995) 'Common Wealth and the Communist party and the 1945 general election', *Contemporary Record*, 9, 1: 62–79.

Campbell, J. (1987) *Nye Bevan and the Mirage of British Socialism*, London: Weidenfeld and Nicolson.

Carruthers, S. (1990) ' "Manning the Factories": propaganda and policy on the employment of women, 1939–1947', *History*, 75, 244: 232–56.

Cockett, R. (1995) *Thinking the Unthinkable: Think Tanks and the Economic Counter-Revolution 1931–83*, London: Fontana.

Corfield, T. (1996) 'Why Chamberlain really fell', *History Today*, 46, 12: 22–8.

Crosby, T. (1986) *The Impact of Civilian Evacuation in the Second World War*, London: Croom Helm.

Cutler, T., Williams, K. and Williams, J. (1986) *Keynes, Beveridge and Beyond*, London: Routledge and Kegan Paul.

Dutton, D. (1997a) *Anthony Eden: A Life and a Reputation*, London: Arnold.

—— (1997b edn) *British Politics since 1945*, Oxford: Blackwell.

Feiling, K. (1970 edn) *The Life of Neville Chamberlain*, London: Macmillan.

Fielding, S. (1992) 'What did "the people" want? The meaning of the 1945 general election', *Historical Journal*, 35, 3: 623–39.

—— (1995) 'The second world war and popular radicalism: the significance of the "movement away from party" ', *History*, 80, 258: 38–58.

——(1997) 'The good war: 1939–1945', in N. Tiratsoo (ed.) *From Blitz to Blair: A New History of Britain since 1939*, London: Weidenfeld and Nicolson.

Fielding, S., Thompson, P. and Tiratsoo, N. (1995) ' *"England Arise!": The Labour Party and Popular Politics in 1940s Britain*, Manchester: Manchester University Press.

Finlayson, G. (1994) *Citizen, State and Social Welfare in Britain, 1830–1990*, Oxford: Clarendon Press.

Foot, M. (1975 edn) *Aneurin Bevan 1897–1945*, London: Granada.

Gilbert, M. (1983) *Winston S. Churchill*, Vol. VI, *Finest Hour 1939–1941*, London: Heinemann.

—— (1986) *Winston S. Churchill*, Vol. VII, *Road to Victory 1941–1945*, London: Heinemann.

Goldsmith, M. (1946) *Women and the Future*, London: Lindsay Drummond.

Gosden, P. (1976) *Education in the Second World War: A Study in Policy and Administration*, London: Methuen.

Harris, J. (1977) *William Beveridge: A Biography*, Oxford: Oxford University Press.

—— (1981) 'Social policy-making in Britain during the second world war', in W. Mommsen (ed.) *The Emergence of the Welfare State in Britain and Germany*, London: Croom Helm.

—— (1986) 'Political ideas and the debate on state welfare 1940–45', in H. Smith (ed.) *War and Social Change: British Society in the Second World War*, Manchester: Manchester University Press.

—— (1992) 'War and social history: Britain and the home front during the second world war', *Contemporary European History*, 1, 1: 17–35.

—— (1994) 'Great Britain: the people's war?', in D. Reynolds, W. Kimball and A. O. Chubarian (eds) *Allies at War*, London: Macmillan.

—— (1996) ' "Contract" and "Citizenship" ', in D. Marquand and A. Seldon (eds) *The Ideas that Shaped Post-War Britain*, London: Fontana.

Harris, K. (1982) *Attlee*, London: Weidenfeld and Nicolson.

Harrisson, T. (1976) *Living Through the Blitz*, London: Collins.

Hayek, F. A. (1944) *The Road to Serfdom*, London: Routledge.

Hennessy, P. (1989) *Whitehall*, London: Secker and Warburg.

—— (1992) *Never Again: Britain 1945–1951*, London: Jonathan Cape.

Holmes, C. (1988) *John Bull's Island: Immigration and British Society, 1871–1971*, London: Macmillan.

—— (1990) 'Enemy aliens?', *History Today*, 40, 9: 25–31.

Jefferys, K. (1987) 'British politics and social policy during the second world war', *The Historical Journal*, 30, 1: 123–44.

—— (1991) *The Churchill Coalition and Wartime Politics 1940–1945*, Manchester: Manchester University Press.

—— (1994) *War and Reform: British Politics During the Second World War*, Manchester: Manchester University Press.

Kandiah, M. D. (1995) 'The Conservative party and the 1945 general election', *Contemporary Record*, 9, 1: 22–47.

Kavanagh, D. and Morris, P. (1994) *Consensus Politics from Attlee to Major*, Oxford: Blackwell.

Kirkham, P. (1995) 'Beauty and duty: keeping up the (home) front', in P. Kirkham and D. Thoms (eds) *War Culture: Social Change and Changing Experience in World War Two Britain*, London: Lawrence and Wishart.

Kochan, M. (1983) *Britain's Internees in the Second World War*, London: Macmillan.

Lafitte, F. (1988 edn) *The Internment of Aliens*, London: Libris.

Lewis, P. (1986) *A People's War*, London: Thames Methuen.

Lowe, R. (1990) 'The second world war, consensus and the foundation of the welfare state', *Twentieth Century British History*, 1, 2: 152–82.

Lin, P. Y. (1996) 'National identity and social mobility: class, empire and the British government's overseas evacuation of schoolchildren during the second world war', *Twentieth Century British History*, 7, 3: 310–44.

McCallum, R. B. and Readman, A. (1947) *The General Election of 1945*, Oxford: Oxford University Press.

Mackay, R. (1999) *The Test of War: Inside Britain 1939–45*, London: UCL Press.

Mackenzie, S. P. (1992) *Politics and Military Morale: Current Affairs and Citizenship Education in the British Army 1914–1950*, Oxford: Clarendon Press.

Macleod, I. (1961) *Neville Chamberlain*, London: Frederick Muller.

MacLeod, R. (1986) 'The promise of full employment', in H. Smith (ed.) *War and Social Change: British Society in the Second World War*, Manchester: Manchester University Press.

Macnicol, J. (1986) 'The effect of the evacuation of schoolchildren on official attitudes to state intervention', in H. Smith (ed.) *War and Social Change: British Society in the Second World War*, Manchester: Manchester University Press.

Marquand, D. (1988) *The Unprincipled Society: New Demands and Old Politics*, London: Fontana.

Marshall, T. H. (1950) *Citizenship and Social Class and Other Essays*, Cambridge: Cambridge University Press.

—— (1963) 'The welfare state and the affluent society', in *Sociology at the Crossroads and Other Essays*, London: Heinemann

Marwick, A. (1968) *Britain in the Century of Total War*, London: Bodley Head.

—— (1974) *War and Social Change in the Twentieth Century*, London: Macmillan.

—— (1976) 'People's war and top people's peace', in A. Sked and C. Cook (eds) *Crisis and Controversy: Essays in Honour of A. J. P. Taylor*, London: Macmillan.

—— (ed.) (1988) *Total War and Social Change*, London: Macmillan.

Mason, T., and Thompson, P. (1991) ' "Reflections on a revolution?", the political mood in wartime Britain', in N. Tiratsoo (ed.) *The Attlee Years*, London: Pinter.

Miliband, R. (1972 edn) *Parliamentary Socialism: A Study in the Politics of Labour*, London: Merlin Press.

Mitchell, J. (1974) *Psychoanalysis and Feminism*, Harmondsworth: Penguin.

Morgan, D. and Evans, M. (1993) 'The road to *Nineteen Eighty-Four*: Orwell and the post-war reconstruction of citizenship', in B. Brivati and H. Jones (eds) *What Difference Did the War Make?*, Leicester: Leicester University Press.

Morgan, K. O. (1984) *Labour in Power 1945–51*, Oxford: Oxford University Press.

Mosse, G. L. (1986) 'Two world wars and the myth of the war experience', *Journal of Contemporary History*, 21, 4: 491–513.

Myrdal, A. and Klein, V. (1956) *Women's Two Roles*, London: Routledge and Kegan Paul.

Pimlott, B. (1985) *Hugh Dalton*, London: Jonathan Cape.

—— (ed.) (1986) *The Second World War Diary of Hugh Dalton, 1940–45*, London: Jonathan Cape.

—— (1988) 'The myth of consensus', in L. M. Smith (ed.) *The Making of Britain: Echoes of Greatness*, London: Macmillan.

Ponting, C. (1990) *1940: Myth and Reality*, London: Hamish Hamilton.

—— (1994) *Churchill*, London: Sinclair Stevenson.

Ramsden, J. (1995) 'Winston Churchill and the leadership of the Conservative party, 1940–51', *Contemporary Record*, 9, 1: 99–119.

Riley, D. (1983) *War in the Nursery: Theories of the Child and the Mother*, London: Virago.

Roberts, A. (1992) *The Holy Fox: A Life of Lord Halifax*, London: Papermac.

—— (1994) *Eminent Churchillians*, London: Weidenfeld and Nicolson.

Roberts, D. M. (1976) 'Clement Davies and the fall of Neville Chamberlain, 1939–40', *Welsh History Review*, 8: 188–215.

Robbins, K. (1992) *Churchill*, London: Longman.

Sheridan, D. (ed.) (1991) *Wartime Women: An Anthology of Women's Wartime Writing for Mass-Observation 1937–1945*, London: Mandarin.

Smith, G. (1987) *When Jim Crow Met John Bull: Black American Soldiers in World War II Britain*, London: I. B. Tauris.

Smith, H. (1981) 'The problem of "equal pay for equal work" in Great Britain during world war II', *Journal of Modern History*, 53, 4: 652–72.

—— (1984) 'The womanpower problem in Britain during the second world war', *The Historical Journal*, 27, 4: 925–45.

—— (1986) 'The effect of the war on the status of women', in H. Smith (ed.) *War and Social Change: British Society in the Second World War*, Manchester: Manchester University Press.

—— (1966) *Britain in the Second World War: A Social History*, Manchester: Manchester University Press.

Smith, M. (1990) *British Politics, Society and the State Since the Late Nineteenth Century*, London: Macmillan.

—— (1993) 'The changing nature of the British state 1929–59: the historiography of consensus', in B. Brivati and H. Jones (eds) *What Difference Did the War Make?*, Leicester: Leicester University Press.

Smithies, E. (1982) *Crime in Wartime: A Social History of Crime in World War II*, London: Allen and Unwin.

Summerfield, P. (1984) *Women Workers in the Second World War: Production and Patriarchy in Conflict*, London: Croom Helm.

—— (1985) 'Mass Observation: social history or social movement?', *Journal of Contemporary History*, 20, 3: 439–52.

—— (1986) 'The "levelling of class" ', in H. Smith (ed.) *War and Social Change: British Society in the Second World War*, Manchester: Manchester University Press.

—— (1988) 'Women, war and social change: women in Britain in world war II', in A. Marwick (ed.) *Total War and Social Change*, London: Macmillan.

—— (1993) 'Approaches to women and social change in the second world war', in B. Brivati and H. Jones (eds) *What Difference Did the War Make?*, Leicester: Leicester University Press.

Thom, D. (1986) 'The 1944 Education Act: the "art of the possible"?', in H.
Smith (ed.) *War and Social Change*, Manchester: Manchester University Press.
Titmuss, R. M. (1950) *Problems of Social Policy*, London: HMSO and Longmans.
—— (1958) *Essays on 'the Welfare State'*, London: George Allen and Unwin.
Welshman, J. (1998) 'Evacuation and social policy during the second world
war: myth and reality', *Twentieth Century British History*, 9, 1: 28–53.
Williams, G. (1945) *Women and Work*, London: Nicholson and Watson.
Winter, J. M. (1986) 'The demographic consequences of the war', in H. Smith
(ed.) *War and Social Change*, Manchester: Manchester University Press.

Wartime economy

Aldcroft, D. H. (1986) *The British Economy*, Vol. I, *The Years of Turmoil 1920–51*,
Brighton: Wheatsheaf.
Barnett, C. (1987) *The Audit of War: The Illusion and Reality of Britain as a Great
Nation*, London: Macmillan.
Booth, A. (1983) 'The "Keynesian Revolution" in economic policy-making',
Economic History Review, 36, 1: 103–23.
—— (1984) 'Defining a "Keynesian Revolution" ', *Economic History Review*, 37,
2: 263–7.
—— (1985) 'The "Keynesian Revolution" and economic policy-making: a
reply', *Economic History Review*, 38, 1: 101–6.
—— (1989) *British Economic Policy, 1931–49: was there a Keynesian Revolution?*
Brighton: Wheatsheaf.
Brooke, S. (1989) 'Revisionists and fundamentalists: the Labour Party and
economic policy during the second world war', *The Historical Journal*, 32, 1:
157–75.
Cairncross, A. (1987) *Years of Recovery: British Economic Policy 1945–51*, London:
Methuen.
—— (1995) 'Economists in wartime', *Contemporary European History*, 4, 1: 19–36.
Cairncross A. and Watts, N. (1989) *The Economic Section 1939–61: A Study in
Economic Advising*, London: Routledge.
Chester, D. N. (1951) *Lessons of the British War Economy*, Cambridge: Cambridge
University Press.
Clarke, R. W. B. (1982) *Anglo-American Collaboration in War and Peace 1942–9*,
Oxford: Clarendon Press.
Edgerton, D. (1992) 'Whatever happened to the British warfare state? The
Ministry of Supply, 1945–51', in H. Mercer, N. Rollings and J. Tomlinson
(eds) *Labour Governments and Private Industry: The Experience of 1945–51*, Edin-
burgh: Edinburgh University Press.
Gowing, M. (1972) 'The organisation of manpower in Britain during the second
world war', *Journal of Contemporary History*, 7, 2: 147–67.
Hancock, W. K. and Gowing, M. M. (1949) *British War Economy*, London:
HMSO.

Harrison, M. (1988) 'Resource mobilisation for world war II: the USA, UK, USSR and Germany, 1938–45', *Economic History Review*, 41, 2: 171–92.

Hobsbawm, E. (1993) 'Britain: a comparative view', in B. Brivati and H. Jones (eds) *What Difference Did the War Make?*, Leicester: Leicester University Press.

Howlett, W. P. (1992) *New Light Through Old Windows: A New Perspective on the British Economy in the Second World War*, London School of Economics working papers.

Johnman, L. (1991) 'The Labour party and industrial policy, 1940–5', in N. Tiratsoo (ed.) *The Attlee Years*, London: Pinter.

Mercer, H. (1991) 'The Labour governments of 1945–51 and private industry', in N. Tiratsoo (ed.) *The Attlee Years*, London: Pinter.

Mercer, H., Rollings, N. and Tomlinson, J. (eds) *Labour Governments and Private Industry: The Experience of 1945–51*, Edinburgh: Edinburgh University Press.

Middlemas, K. (1986) *Power, Competition and the State*, Vol. I, *Britain in Search of Balance, 1940–61*, London: Macmillan.

Milward, A. S. (1977) *War, Economy and Society 1939–45*, London: Allen Lane.

—— (1984 edn) *The Economic Effects of the Two World Wars on Britain*, London: Macmillan.

Peden, G. C. (1983) 'Sir Richard Hopkins and the "Keynesian Revolution" in employment policy, 1929–45', *Economic History Review*, 36, 2: 281–96.

Pope, R. (1991) *War and Society in Britain, 1899–1948*, London: Longman.

Rollings, N. (1985) 'The "Keynesian Revolution" and economic policy-making: a comment', *Economic History Review*, 38, 1: 95–106.

—— (1992) ' "The Reichstag method of governing"? The Attlee governments and permanent economic controls', in H. Mercer, N. Rollings and J. Tomlinson (eds) *Labour Governments and Private Industry: The Experience of 1945–51*, Edinburgh: Edinburgh University Press.

Sayers, R. S. (1983) '1941 – the first Keynesian budget', in C. Feinstein (ed.) *The Managed Economy: Essays in British Economic Policy Performance Since 1929*, Oxford: Oxford University Press.

Tiratsoo, N. and Tomlinson, J. (1993) *Industrial Efficiency and State Intervention: Labour 1939–51*, London: Routledge.

Tomlinson, J. (1984) 'A "Keynesian Revolution" in economic policy-making?', *Economic History Review*, 37, 2: 258–67.

—— (1985) *British Macroeconomic Policy Since 1940*, Beckenham: Croom Helm.

—— (1987) *Employment Policy: The Crucial Years 1939–45*, Oxford: Clarendon.

—— (1993) 'Mr Attlee's supply-side socialism', *Economic History Review*, 46, 1: 1–22.

Press, propaganda and culture

Aldgate, T. and Richards, J. (1986) *Britain Can Take It: British Cinema in the Second World War*, Oxford: Basil Blackwell.

Balfour, M. (1979) *Propaganda in War 1939–1945: Organisation, Policies and Publics in Britain and Germany*, London: Routledge and Kegan Paul.

Briggs, A. (1995 edn) *The History of Broadcasting in the United Kingdom*, Vol. III, *The War of Words*, Oxford: Oxford University Press.

Calder, A. (1991) *The Myth of the Blitz*, London: Jonathan Cape.

Chapman, J. (1998) *The British at War: Cinema, State and Propaganda 1939–1945*, London: I. B. Tauris.

Christie, I. (ed.) (1994) *Powell and Pressburger: The Life and Death of Colonel Blimp*, London: Faber and Faber.

Coultass, C. (1984) 'British feature films and the second world war', *Journal of Contemporary History*, 19, 1: 7–22.

—— (1989) *Images for Battle: British Film and the Second World War, 1939–1945*, London and Toronto: Associated University Presses.

Cudlipp, H. (1953) *Publish and be Damned: the Astonishing Story of the Daily Mirror*, London: Andrew Dakers.

Curran, J. and Seaton, J. (1997 edn) *Power Without Responsibility: The Press and Broadcasting in Britain*, London: Routledge.

Darracott, J. and Loftus, B. (1985) *Second World War Posters*, London: Imperial War Museum.

Dickinson, M. and Street, S. (1985) *Cinema and Society: The Film Industry and Government, 1927–84*, London: BFI.

Douglas, R. (1990) *The World War 1939–1945: The Cartoonists Vision*, London: Routledge.

Harman, N. (1980) *Dunkirk: The Necessary Myth*, London: Hodder and Stoughton.

Hewison, R. (1995) *Culture and Consensus: England, Art and Politics Since 1940*, London: Methuen.

Kimble, P. (1942) *Newspaper Reading in the Third Year of the War*, London: George Allen and Unwin.

King, C. (1970) *With Malice Toward None: A War Diary*, (ed. W. Armstrong), London: Sidgwick and Jackson.

Knightley, P. (1975) *The First Casualty: The War Correspondent as Hero, Propagandist, and Myth Maker from the Crimea to Vietnam*, London: Andre Deutsch.

Koss, S. (1984) *The Rise and Fall of the Political Press in Britain*, Vol. II, *The Twentieth Century*, London: Hamish Hamilton.

McKibbin, R. (1998) *Classes and Cultures: England 1918–1951*, Oxford: Oxford University Press.

McLaine, I. (1979) *Ministry of Morale: Home Front Morale and the Ministry of Information in World War II*, London: Allen and Unwin.

Margach, J. (1978) *The Abuse of Power: The War Between Downing Street and the Media from Lloyd George to Callaghan*, London: W. H. Allen.

Murphy, R. (1992) *Realism and Tinsel: Cinema and Society in Britain 1939–49*, London: Routledge.

Nicholas, S. (1995) ' "Sly demagogues" and wartime radio: J. B. Priestley and the BBC, 1939–1945', *Twentieth Century British History*, 6, 3: 247–66.

—— (1996) *The Echo of War: Home Front Propaganda and the Wartime BBC, 1939–45*, Manchester: Manchester University Press.

Pronay, N. and Spring, D. W. (eds) (1982) *Propaganda, Politics and Film 1918–45*, London: Macmillan.

Scannell, P. and Cardiff, D. (1987) 'The BBC and national unity', in J. Curran, A. Smith and P. Wingate (eds) *Impacts and Influences: Essays on Media Power in the Twentieth Century*, London: Methuen.

Seaton, J. (1987) 'The Holocaust: a case study of atrocities and the media', in J. Seaton and B. Pimlott (eds) *The Media in British Politics*, Aldershot: Gower.

Short, K. R. M. (ed.) (1983) *Film and Radio Propaganda in World War II*, London: Croom Helm.

Smith, A. C. H., Immirzi, E. and Blackwell, T. (1975) *Paper Voices: The Popular Press and Social Change, 1935–1965*, London: Chatto and Windus.

Stammers, N. (1983) *Civil Liberties in Britain During the Second World War: A Political Study*, London: Croom Helm.

Taylor, P. M. (ed.) (1988) *Britain and the Cinema in the Second World War*, London: Macmillan.

Wenden, D. J. (1996) 'Churchill, radio and cinema', in R. Blake and Wm. Roger Louis (eds) *Churchill*, Oxford: Oxford University Press.

Wartime strategy

Barnett, C. (1983) *The Desert Generals*, London: Allen and Unwin.

Beckett, I. (1992) 'Wavell', in J. Keegan (ed.) *Churchill's Generals*, London: Warner Books.

Butler, J. R. M. (ed.) *Grand Strategy – British History of the Second World War – UK Military Series*:

—— (1956) Vol. I, N. Gibbs, London: HMSO.

—— (1957) Vol. II, J. R. M. Butler, London: HMSO.

—— (1964) Vol. III, part 1, J. M. A. Gwyer, London: HMSO.

—— (1964) Vol. III, part 2, J. R. M. Butler, London: HMSO.

—— (1972) Vol. IV, M. Howard, London: HMSO.

—— (1956) Vol. V, J. Ehrman, London: HMSO.

—— (1956) Vol. VI, J. Ehrman, London: HMSO.

Carver, M. (1996) 'Churchill and the Defence Chiefs', in R. Blake and Wm. Roger Louis (eds) *Churchill*, Oxford: Clarendon Press.

Charmley, J. (1993) *Churchill: The End of Glory*, London: Hodder and Stoughton.

Churchill, W. S. *The Second World War*:

—— (1948) Vol. I, *The Gathering Storm*, London: Cassell.

—— (1949) Vol. II, *Their Finest Hour*, London: Cassell.

—— (1950) Vol. III, *The Grand Alliance*, London: Cassell.

—— (1951) Vol. IV, *The Hinge of Fate*, London: Cassell.

Douglas, R. (1981) *From World War to Cold War, 1942–1948*, London: Macmillan.

Edmonds, R. (1991) *The Big Three: Churchill, Roosevelt and Stalin*, London: Hamish Hamilton.

Fraser, D. (1982) *Alanbrooke*, London: Collins.

Grigg, J. (1985 edn) *1943: The Victory That Never Was*, London: Methuen.

Hamilton, N. (1981) *Monty: The Making of a General, 1887–1942*, London: Hamish Hamilton.

—— (1983) *Monty: Master of the Battlefield, 1942–1944*, London: Hamish Hamilton.

—— (1986) *Monty: The Field Marshall, 1944–1976*, London: Hamish Hamilton.

Hastings, M. (1984) *Overlord: D-Day and the Battle for Normandy 1944*, London: Michael Joseph.

Irving, D. (1987) *Churchill's War*, Vol. I, *The Struggle for Power*, Bullsbrook, W.A., Australia: Veritas Publishing Co.

Keegan, J. (ed.) (1992) *Churchill's Generals*, London: Warner Books.

—— (1995) *The Battle for History: Re-fighting World War II*, London: Hutchinson.

—— (1996) 'Churchill's strategy', in R. Blake and Wm. Roger Louis (eds) *Churchill*, Oxford: Clarendon Press.

—— (1997 edn) *The Second World War*, London: Pimlico.

Lamb, R. (1993) *Churchill as War Leader: Right or Wrong?*, London: Bloomsbury.

Liddell Hart, B. (1969) 'The military strategist', in A. J. P. Taylor, R. Rhodes James, J. H. Plumb, B. Liddell Hart and A. Storr, *Churchill: Four Faces and the Man*, London: Allen Lane.

—— (1970) *History of the Second World War*, London: Cassell.

Howard, M. (1992 edn) *Strategic Deception in the Second World War*, London: Pimlico.

Overy, R. (1980) *The Air War, 1939–1945*, London: Europa.

—— (1996 edn) *Why the Allies Won*, London: Pimlico.

Parker, R. A. C. (1990) *Struggle for Survival: The History of the Second World War*, Oxford: Oxford University Press.

Reynolds, D. (1985) 'Churchill and the British "decision" to fight on in 1940: right policy, wrong reasons', in R. Langhorne (ed.) *Diplomacy and Intelligence During the Second World War*, Cambridge: Cambridge University Press.

—— (1991) *Britannia Overruled: British Policy and World Power in the Twentieth Century*, London: Longman.

Weinberg, G. L. (1994) *A World at Arms: A Global History of World War II*, Cambridge: Cambridge University Press.

Woodward, L. *British Foreign Policy in the Second World War*:

—— (1970) Vol. I, London: HMSO.

—— (1971) Vol. II, London: HMSO.

—— (1972) Vol. III, London: HMSO.

—— (1975) Vol. IV, London: HMSO.

——(1976) Vol. V, London: HMSO.

Index